W9-CDU-406

The Book of Hallowe'en

The Origin and History of Halloween

By

Ruth Edna Kelley, A.M.

Originally published 1919

Table of Contents

Dedication

TO MY MOTHER AND THE MEMORY
OF MY FATHER

who inspired and encouraged me in the
writing of this book.

Preface

THIS book is intended to give the reader an account of the origin and history of Hallowe'en, how it absorbed some customs belonging to other days in the year,—such as May Day, Midsummer, and Christmas. The context is illustrated by selections from ancient and modern poetry and prose, related to Hallowe'en ideas.   Those who wish suggestions for reading, recitations, plays, and parties, will find the lists in the appendix useful, in addition to the books on entertainments and games to be found in any public library.

Special acknowledgment is made to Messrs. E.P. Dutton and Company for permission to use the poem entitled "Hallowe'en" from "The Spires of Oxford and Other Poems," by W. M. Letts; to Messrs. Longmans, Green and Company for the poem "Pomona," by William Morris; and to the Editors of The Independent for the use of five poems.

RUTH EDNA KELLEY.
Lynn, 1919.

Chapter I. Sun-Worship. The Sources Of Hallowe'en

IF we could ask one of the old-world pagans whom he revered as his greatest gods, he would be sure to name among them the sun-god; calling him Apollo if he were a Greek; if an Egyptian, Horus or Osiris; if of Norway, Sol; if of Peru, Bochica. As the sun in the center of the physical universe, so all primitive peoples made it the hub about which their religion revolved, nearly always believing it a living person to whom they could say prayers and offer sacrifices, who directed their lives and destinies, and could even snatch men from earthly existence to dwell for a time with him, as it draws the water from lakes and seas.   In believing this they followed an instinct of all early peoples, a desire to make persons of the great powers of nature, such as the world of growing things, mountains and water, the sun, moon, and stars; and a wish for these gods they had made to take an interest in and be part of their daily life. The next step was making stories about them to account for what was seen; so arose myths and legends.

The sun has always marked out work-time and rest, divided the year into winter idleness, seed-time, growth, and harvest; it has always been responsible for all the beauty and goodness of the earth; it is itself splendid to look upon. It goes away and stays longer and longer, leaving the land in cold and gloom; it returns bringing the long fair days and resurrection of spring. A Japanese legend tells how the hidden sun was lured out by an image made of a

copper plate with saplings radiating from it like
sunbeams, and a fire kindled, dancing, and prayers;
and round the earth in North America the
Cherokees believed they brought the sun back upon
its northward path by the same means of rousing its
curiosity, so that it would come out to see its
counterpart and find out what was going on.

All the more important church festivals are
survivals of old rites to the sun. "How many times
the Church has decanted the new wine of
Christianity into the old bottles of heathendom."
Yule-tide, the pagan Christmas, celebrated the sun's
turning north, and the old midsummer holiday is
still kept in Ireland and on the Continent as St.
John's Day by the lighting of bonfires and a dance
about them from east to west as the sun appears to
move. The pagan Hallowe'en at the end of summer
was a time of grief for the decline of the sun's glory,
as well as a harvest festival of thanksgiving to him
for having ripened the grain and fruit, as we
formerly had husking-bees when the ears had been
garnered, and now keep our own Thanksgiving by
eating of our winter store in praise of God who
gives us our increase.

Pomona, the Roman goddess of fruit, lends
us the harvest element of Hallowe'en; the Celtic day
of "summer's end" was a time when spirits, mostly
evil, were abroad; the gods whom Christ dethroned
joined the ill-omened throng; the Church festivals
of All Saints' and All Souls' coming at the same
time of year—the first of November—contributed
the idea of the return of the dead; and the Teutonic
May Eve assemblage of witches brought its hags
and their attendant beasts to help celebrate the night
of October 31st.

Chapter II. The Celts: Their Religion And Festivals

THE first reference to Great Britain in European annals of which we know was the statement in the fifth century B.C. of the Greek historian Herodotus, that Phoenician sailors went to the British Isles for tin. He called them the "Tin Islands." The people with whom these sailors traded must have been Celts, for they were the first inhabitants of Britain who worked in metal instead of stone. The Druids were priests of the Celts centuries before Christ came. There is a tradition in Ireland that they first arrived there in 270 B.C., seven hundred years before St. Patrick. The account of them written by Julius Caesar half a century before Christ speaks mainly of the Celts of Gaul, dividing them into two ruling classes who kept the people almost in a state of slavery; the knights, who wages war, and the Druids who had charge of worship and sacrifices, and were in addition physicians, historians, teachers, scientists, and judges.

Caesar says that this cult originated in Britain, and was transferred to Gaul. Gaul and Britain had one religion and one language, and might even have one king, so that what Caesar wrote of Gallic Druids must have been true of British.

The Celts worshipped spirits of forest and stream, and feared the powers of evil, as did the Greeks and all other early races. Very much of their primitive belief has been kept so that to Scotch,

Irish, and Welsh peasantry brooks, hills, dales, and rocks abound in tiny supernatural beings, who may work them good or evil, lead them astray by flickering lights, or charm them into seven years' servitude unless they are bribed to show favor.

The name "Druid" is derived from the Celtic word "druidh," meaning "sage," connected with the Greek word for oak, "drus,"

"The rapid oak-tree—
Before him heaven and earth quake:
Stout door-keeper against the foe.
In every land his name is mine."
—TALIESIN: *Battle of the Trees.*

for the oak was held sacred by them as a symbol of the omnipotent god, upon whom they depended for life like the mistletoe growing upon it. Their ceremonies were held in oak-groves.

Later from their name a word meaning "magician" was formed, showing that these priests had gained the reputation of being dealers in magic.

"The Druid followed him and suddenly, as we are told, struck him with a druidic wand, or according to one version, flung at him a tuft of grass over which he had pronounced a druidical incantation."
—O'CURRY: *Ancient Irish.*

They dealt in symbols, common objects to which was given by the interposition of spirits, meaning to signify certain facts, and power to produce certain effects. Since they were tree-worshippers, trees and plants were thought to have peculiar powers.

Caesar provides them with a galaxy of Roman divinities, Mercury, Mars, Jupiter, and Minerva, who of course were worshipped under their native names. Their chief god was Baal, of whom they believed the sun the visible emblem. They represented him by lowlier tokens, such as circles and wheels. The trefoil, changed into a figure composed of three winged feet radiating from a center, represented the swiftness of the sun's journey. The cross too was a symbol of the sun, being the appearance of its light shining upon dew or stream, making to the half-closed eye little bright crosses. One form of the cross was the swastika.

To Baal they made sacrifices of criminals or prisoners of war, often burning them alive in wicker images. These bonfires lighted on the hills were meant to urge the god to protect and bless the crops and herds. From the appearance of the victims sacrificed in them, omens were taken that foretold the future. The gods and other supernatural powers in answer to prayer were thought to signify their will by omens, and also by the following methods: the ordeal, in which the innocence or guilt of a person was shown by the way the god permitted him to endure fire or other torture; exorcisms, the driving out of demons by saying mysterious words or names over them. Becoming skilled in interpreting the will of the gods, the Druids came to be known as prophets.

> "O Deirdre, terrible child,
> For thee, red star of our ruin,
> Great weeping shall be in Eri—
> Woe, woe, and a breach in Ulla.

* * * * * *

"Thy feet shall trample the mighty
Yet stumble on heads thou lovest."
—TODHUNTER: *Druid song of Cathvah.*

They kept their lore for the most part a
secret, forbidding it to be written, passing it down
by word of mouth. They taught the immortality of
the soul, that it passed from one body to another at
death.

"If, as those Druids taught, which kept the British
rites,
And dwelt in darksome groves, there counselling
with sprites,
When these our souls by death our bodies do
forsake
They instantly again do other bodies take—-"
—DRAYTON: *Polyolbion.*

They believed that on the last night of the
old year (October 31st) the lord of death gathered
together the souls of all those who had died in the
passing year and had been condemned to live in the
bodies of animals to decree what forms they should
inhabit for the next twelve months. He could be
coaxed to give lighter sentences by gifts and
prayers.
The badge of the initiated Druid was a glass
ball reported to be made in summer of the spittle of
snakes, and caught by the priests as the snakes
tossed it into the air.

"And the potent adder-stone

Gender'd 'fore the autumnal moon
When in undulating twine
The foaming snakes prolific join."
—MASON: *Caractacus.*

It was real glass, blown by the Druids themselves. It was supposed to aid the wearer in winning lawsuits and securing the favor of kings.

An animal sacred to the Druids was the cat.

"A slender black cat reclining on a chain of old silver" guarded treasure in the old days. For a long time cats were dreaded by the people because they thought human beings had been changed to that form by evil means.

The chief festivals of the Druids fell on four days, celebrating phases of the sun's career. Fires of sacrifice were lighted especially at spring and midsummer holidays, by exception on November 1st.

May Day and November Day were the more important, the beginning and end of summer, yet neither equinoxes nor solstices.

The time was divided then not according to sowing and reaping, but by the older method of reckoning from when the herds were turned out to pasture in the spring and brought into the fold again at the approach of winter—by a pastoral rather than an agricultural people.

On the night before Beltaine ("Baal-fire"), the first of May, fires were burned to Ball to celebrate the return of the sun bringing summer. Before sunrise the houses were decked with garlands to gladden the sun when he appeared; a rite which has survived in "going maying." The May-Day fires were used for purification. Cattle were singed by being led near the flames, and sometimes bled that their blood might be offered as a sacrifice for a prosperous season.

> "When lo! a flame,
> A wavy flame of ruddy light
> Leaped up, the farmyard fence above.
> And while his children's shout rang high,
> His cows the farmer slowly drove
> Across the blaze,—he knew not why."
> —KICKHAM:*St. John's Eve.*

A cake was baked in the fire with one piece blacked with charcoal. Whoever got the black piece was thereby marked for sacrifice to Baal, so that, as the ship proceeded in safety after Jonah was cast overboard, the affairs of the group about the May-Eve fire might prosper when it was purged of the one whom Baal designated by lot. Later only the symbol of offering was used, the victim being forced to leap thrice over the flames.

In history it was the day of the coming of good. Partholon, the discoverer and promoter of Ireland, came thither from the other world to stay three hundred years. The gods themselves, the deliverers of Ireland, first arrived there "through the air" on May Day.

June 21st, the day of the summer solstice, the height of the sun's power, was marked by midnight fires of joy and by dances. These were believed to strengthen the sun's heat. A blazing wheel to represent the sun was rolled down hill.

> "A happy thought.
> Give me this cart-wheel.

I'll have it tied with ropes and smeared
with pitch,
And when it's lighted, I will roll it down
The steepest hillside."
—HAUPTMANN:*Sunken Bell.*
(Lewisohn trans.)

Spirits were believed to be abroad, and
torches were carried about the fields to protect them
from invasion. Charms were tried on that night with
seeds of fern and hemp, and dreams were believed
to be prophetic.
Lugh, in old Highland speech "the summer sun"

"The hour may hither drift
When at the last, amid the o'erwearied Shee—
Weary of long delight and deathless joys—
One you shall love may fade before your eyes,
Before your eyes may fade, and be as mist
Caught in the sunny hollow of Lu's hand,
Lord of the Day."
—SHARP: *Immortal Hour.*

had for father one of the gods and for
mother the daughter of a chief of the enemy. Hence
he possessed some good and some evil tendencies.
He may be the Celtic Mercury, for they were alike
skilled in magic and alchemy, in deception,
successful in combats with demons, the bringers of
new strength and cleansing to the nation. He said
farewell to power on the first of August, and his
foster-mother had died on that day, so then it was he
set his feast-day. The occasion was called
"Lugnasad," "the bridal of Lugh" and the earth,
whence the harvest should spring. It was celebrated

by the offering of the first fruits of harvest, and by races and athletic sports. In Meath, Ireland, this continued down into the nineteenth century, with dancing and horse-racing the first week of August.

Chapter III. Samhain

ON November first was Samhain ("summer's end").

> "Take my tidings:
> Stags contend;
> Snows descend—
> Summer's end!
> "A chill wind raging,
> The sun low keeping,
> Swift to set
> O'er seas high sweeping.
> "Dull red the fern;
> Shapes are shadows;
> Wild geese mourn
> O'er misty meadows.
> "Keen cold limes each weaker wing,
> Icy times—
> Such I sing!
> Take my tidings."
> —GRAVES: *First Winter Song.*

Then the flocks were driven in, and men first had leisure after harvest toil. Fires were built as a thanksgiving to Baal for harvest. The old fire on the altar was quenched before the night of October 31st, and the new one made, as were all sacred fires, by friction. It was called "forced-fire." A wheel and a spindle were used: the wheel, the sun symbol, was turned from east to west, sunwise. The sparks were caught in tow, blazed upon the altar, and were passed on to light the hilltop fires. The new fire was given next morning, New Year's Day, by the priests to the people to light their hearths, where all fires had been extinguished. The blessed fire was thought to protect the year through the home it warmed. In Ireland the altar was Tlactga, on the hill of Ward in Meath, where sacrifices, especially black sheep, were burnt in the new fire. From the death struggles and look of the creatures omens for the future year were taken.

The year was over, and the sun's life of a year was done. The Celts thought that at this time the sun fell a victim for six months to the powers of winter darkness. In Egyptian mythology one of the sun-gods, Osiris, was lsain at a banquet by his brother Sitou, the god of darkness. On the anniversary of the murder, the first day of winter, no Egyptian would begin any new business for fear of bad luck, since the spirit of evil was then in power.

From the idea that the sun suffered from his enemies on this day grew the association of Samhain with death.

"The melancholy days are come, the saddest of the year,
Of wailing winds, and naked woods, and meadows brown and sere.
Heaped in the hollows of the grove, the wither'd leaves lie dead;
They rustle to the eddying gust, and to the rabbit's tread.
The robin and the wren are flown, and from the shrub the jay
And from the wood-top calls the crow, through all the gloomy day.
"The wind-flower and the violet, they perished long

ago,
And the wild rose and the orchis died amid the
summer glow:
But on the hill the golden-rod, and the aster in the
wood,
And the yellow sun-flower by the brook in autumn
beauty stood,
Till fell the frost from the cold clear heaven, as falls
the plague on men,
And the brightness of their smile was gone from
upland, glade, and glen."
        —BRYANT: *Death of the Flowers.*

In the same state as those who are dead, are
those who have never lived, dwelling right in the
world, but invisible to most mortals at most times.
Seers could see them at any time, and if very many
were abroad at once others might get a chance to
watch them too.

> "There is a world in which we dwell,
> And yet a world invisible.
> And do not think that naught can be
> Save only what with eyes ye see:
> I tell ye that, this very hour,
> Had but your sight a spirit's power,
> Ye would be looking, eye to eye,
> At a terrific company."
> —COXE: *Hallowe'en.*

These supernatural spirits ruled the dead.
There were two classes: the Tuatha De Danann,
"the people of the goddess Danu," gods of light and
life; and spirits of darkness and evil. The Tuatha
had their chief seat on the Isle of Man, in the middle

of the Irish Sea, and brought under their power the islands about them. On a Midsummer Day they vanquished the Fir Bolgs and gained most of Ireland, by the battle of Moytura.

A long time afterwards—perhaps 1000 B.C.—the Fomor, sea-demons, after destroying nearly all their enemies by plagues, exacted from those remaining, as tribute, "a third part of their corn, a third part of their milk, and a third part of their children." This tax was paid on Samhain. It was on the week before Samhain that the Fomor landed upon Ireland. On the eve of Samhain the gods met them in the second battle of Moytura, and they were driven back into the ocean.

As Tigernmas, a mythical king of Ireland, was sacrificing "the firstlings of every issue, and the scions of every clan" to Crom Croich, the king idol, and lay prostrate before the image, he and three-fourths of his men mysteriously disappeared.

"Then came
Tigernmas, the prince of Tara yonder
On Hallowe'en with many hosts.
A cause of grief to them was the deed.
Dead were the men
Of Bamba's host, without happy strength
Around Tigernmas, the destructive man of the
north,
From the worship of Crom Cruaich. 'Twas no luck
for them.
For I have learnt,
Except one-fourth of the keen Gaels,
Not a man alive—lasting the snare!
Escaped without death in his mouth."
        —*Dinnsenchus of Mag Slecht* (Meyer

trans.).

This was direct invocation, but the fire rites which were continued so long afterwards were really only worshipping the sun by proxy, in his nearest likeness, fire.

Samhain was then a day sacred to the death of the sun, on which had been paid a sacrifice of death to evil powers. Though overcome at Moytura evil was ascendant at Samhain. Methods of finding out the will of spirits and the future naturally worked better then, charms and invocations had more power, for the spirits were near to help, if care was taken not to anger them, and due honors paid.

Chapter IV. Pomona

OPS was the Latin goddess of plenty. Single parts of her province were taken over by various other divinities, among whom was Pomona (*pomorum patrona,* "she who cares for fruits"). She is represented as a maiden with fruit in her arms and a pruning-knife in her hand.

"I am the ancient apple-queen.
As once I was so am I now—
For evermore a hope unseen
Betwixt the blossom and the bough.
"Ah, where's the river's hidden gold!
And where's the windy grave of Troy?
Yet come I as I came of old,
From out the heart of summer's joy."
—MORRIS: *Pomona.*

Many Roman poets told stories about her, the best known being by Ovid, who says that she was wooed by many orchard-gods, but preferred to remain unmarried. Among her suitors was Vertumnus ("the changer"), the god of the turning year, who had charge of the exchange of trade, the turning of river channel, and chiefly of the change in nature from flower to ripe fruit. True to his character he took many forms to gain Pomona's love. Now he was a ploughman (spring), now a fisherman (summer), now a reaper (autumn).

At last he took the likeness of an old woman (winter), and went to gossip with Pomona. After sounding her mind and finding her averse to marriage, the woman pleaded for Vertumnus's success.

> "Is not he the first to have the fruits which
> are thy delight? And does he not hold thy
> gifts in his joyous right hand?"
> —OVID: *Vertumnus and Pomona.*

Then the crone told her the story of Anaxarete who was so cold to her lover Iphis that he hanged himself, and she at the window watching his funeral train pass by was changed to a marble statue. Advising Pomona to avoid such a fate, Vertumnus donned his proper form, that of a handsome young man, and Pomona, moved by the story and his beauty, yielded and became his wife.

Vertumnus had a statue in the Tuscan Way in Rome, and a temple. His festival, the Vortumnalia, was held on the 23d of August, when the summer began to wane. Garlands and garden produce were offered to him.

Pomona had been assigned one of the fifteen flamina, priests whose duty it was to kindle the fire for special sacrifices. She had a grove near Ostia where a harvest festival was held about November first. Not much is known of the ceremonies, but from the similar August holiday much may be deduced. Then the deities of fire and water were propitiated that their disfavor might not ruin the crops. On Pomona's day doubtless thanks was rendered them for their aid to the harvest. An offering of first-fruits was made in August; in November the winter store of nuts and apples was opened. The horses released from toil contended in races.

From Pomona's festival nuts and apples,

from the Druidic Samhain the supernatural element, combined to give later generations the charms and omens from nuts and apples which are made trial of at Hallowe'en.

Chapter V. The Coming Of Christianity. All Saints'. All Souls'.

THE great power which the Druids exercised over their people interfered with the Roman rule of Britain. Converts were being made at Rome. Augustus forbade Romans to become initiated, Tiberius banished the priestly clan and their adherents from Gaul, and Claudius utterly stamped out the belief there, and put to death a Roman knight for wearing the serpent's-egg badge to win a lawsuit. Forbidden to practise their rites in Britain, the Druids fled to the isle of Mona, near the coast of Wales. The Romans pursued them, and in 61 A.D. they were slaughtered and their oak groves cut down. During the next three centuries the cult was stifled to death, and the Christian religion substituted.   It was believed that at Christ's advent the pagan gods either died or were banished.

"The lonely mountains o'er
And the resounding shore
A voice of weeping heard, and loud lament.
From haunted spring and dale,
Edged with poplar pale,
The parting genius is with sighing sent.
With flower-inwoven tresses torn
The nymphs in twilight shade of tangled thickets mourn."
—MILTON: *On the Morning of Christ's Nativity.*

The Christian Fathers explained all oracles and omens by saying that there was something in them, but that they were the work of the evil one. The miraculous power they seemed to possess worked "black magic."

It was a long, hard effort to make men see that their gods had all the time been wrong, and harder still to root out the age-long growth of rite and symbol. But on the old religion might be grafted new names; Midsummer was dedicated to the birth of Saint John; Lugnasad became Lammas. The fires belonging to these times of year were retained, their old significance forgotten or reconsecrated. The rowan, or mountain ash, whose berries had been the food of the Tuatha, now exorcised those very beings. The trefoil signified the Trinity, and the cross no longer the rays of the sun on water, but the cross of Calvary. The fires which had been built to propitiate the god and consume his sacrifices to induce him to protect them were now lighted to protect the people from the same god, declared to be an evil mischief-maker. In time the autumn festival of the Druids became the vigil of All Hallows or All Saints' Day.

All Saints' was first suggested in the fourth century, when the Christians were no longer persecuted, in memory of all the saints, since there were too many for each to have a special day on the church calendar. A day in May was chosen by Pope Boniface IV in 610 for consecrating the Pantheon, the old Roman temple of all the gods, to the Virgin and all the saints and martyrs. Pope Gregory III dedicated a chapel in St. Peter's to the same, and that day was made compulsory in 835 by Pope Gregory IV, as All Saints'. The day was changed

from May to November so that the crowds that
thronged to Rome for the services might be fed
from the harvest bounty. It is celebrated with a
special service in the Greek and Roman churches
and by Episcopalians.

In the tenth century St. Odilo, Bishop of
Cluny, instituted a day of prayer and special masses
for the souls of the dead. He had been told that a
hermit dwelling near a cave

"heard the voices and howlings of devils, which
complained strongly because that the souls of
them that were dead were taken away from
their hands by alms and by prayers."
—DE VORAGINE: *Golden Legend.*

This day became All Souls', and was set for
November 2d.

It is very appropriate that the Celtic festival
when the spirits of the dead and the supernatural
powers held a carnival of triumph over the god of
light, should be followed by All Saints' and All
Souls'. The church holy-days were celebrated by
bonfires to light souls through Purgatory to
Paradise, as they had lighted the sun to his death on
Samhain. On both occasions there were prayers: the
pagan petitions to the lord of death for a pleasant
dwelling-place for the souls of departed friends; and
the Christian for their speedy deliverance from
torture. They have in common the celebrating of
death: the one, of the sun; the other, of mortals: of
harvest: the one, of crops; the other of sacred
memories. They are kept by revelry and joy: first, to
cheer men and make them forget the malign
influences abroad; second, because as the saints in

heaven rejoice over one repentant sinner, we should rejoice over those who, after struggles and sufferings past, have entered into everlasting glory.

"Mother, my Mother, Mother-Country,
Yet were the fields in bud.
And the harvest,—when shall it rise again
Up through the fire and flood?
* * * * *
"Mother, my Mother, Mother-Country,
Was it not all to save
Harvest of bread?—Harvest of men?
And the bright years, wave on wave?
"Search not, search not, my way-worn;
Search neither weald nor wave.
One is their heavy reaping-time
To the earth, that is one wide grave."
—MARKS: *All Souls' Eve.*

Chapter VI. Origin And Character Of Hallowe'en Omens

THE custom of making tests to learn the future comes from the old system of augury from sacrifice. Who sees in the nuts thrown into the fire, turning in the heat, blazing and growing black, the writhing victim of an old-time sacrifice to an idol? Many superstitions and charms were believed to be active at any time, but all those and numerous special ones worked best on November Eve. All the tests of all the Celtic festivals have been allotted to Hallowe'en. Cakes from the May Eve fire, hemp-seed and prophetic dreams from Midsummer, games and sports from Lugnasad have survived in varied forms.

Tests are very often tried blindfold, so that the seeker may be guided by fate. Many are mystic—to evoke apparitions from the past or future. Others are tried with harvest grains and fruits. Because skill and undivided attention is needed to carry them through successfully, many have degenerated into mere contests of skill, have lost their meaning, and become rough games.

Answers are sought to questions about one's future career; chiefly to: when and whom shall I marry? what will be my profession and degree of wealth, and when shall I die?

Chapter VII. Hallowe'en Beliefs And Customs In Ireland

IRELAND has a literature of Hallowe'en, or "Samhain," as it used to be called. Most of it was written between the seventh and the twelfth centuries, but the events were thought to have happened while paganism still ruled in Ireland. The evil powers that came out at Samhain lived the rest of the time in the cave of Cruachan in Connaught, the province which was given to the wicked Fomor after the battle of Moytura. This cave was called the "hell-gate of Ireland," and was unlocked on November Eve to let out spirits and copper-colored birds which killed the farm animals. They also stole babies, leaving in their place changelings, goblins who were old in wickedness while still in the cradle, possessing superhuman cunning and skill in music. One way of getting rid of these demon children was to ill-treat them so that their people would come for them, bringing the right ones back; or one might boil egg-shells in the sight of the changeling, who would declare his demon nature by saying that in his centuries of life he had never seen such a thing before.

Brides too were stolen.

"You shall go with me, newly married bride,
And gaze upon a merrier multitude;
White-armed Nuala and Aengus of the birds,
And Feacra of the hurtling foam, and him
Who is the ruler of the western host,

Finvarra, and the Land of Heart's Desire,
Where beauty has no ebb, decay no flood,
But joy is wisdom, time an endless song."
—YEATS: *Land of Heart's Desire.*

In the first century B.C. lived Ailill and his
queen Medb. As they were celebrating their
Samhain feast in the palace,

"Three days before Samhain at all times,
And three days after, by ancient custom
Did the hosts of high aspiration
Continue to feast for the whole week."
—O'CIARAIN: *Loch Garman.*

they offered a reward to the man who should
tie a bundle of twigs about the feet of a criminal
who had been hanged by the gate. It was dangerous
to go near dead bodies on November Eve, but a
bold young man named Nera dared it, and tied the
twigs successfully. As he turned to go he saw

"the whole of the palace as if on fire before
him, and the heads of the people of it lying on the
ground, and then he thought he saw an army going
into the hill of Cruachan, and he followed after the
army."
—GREGORY: *Cuchulain of Muirthemne.*

The door was shut. Nera was married to a
fairy woman, who betrayed her kindred by sending
Nera to warn King Ailill of the intended attack
upon his palace the next November Eve. Nera bore
summer fruits with him to prove that he had been in
the fairy sid. The next November Eve, when the

doors were opened Ailill entered and discovered the crown, emblem of power, took it away, and plundered the treasury. Nera never returned again to the homes of men.

Another story of about the same time was that of Angus, the son of a Tuatha god, to whom in a dream a beautiful maiden appeared. He wasted away with love for her, and searched the country for a girl who should look like her. At last he saw in a meadow among a hundred and fifty maidens, each with a chain of silver about her neck, one who was like the beauty of his dream. She wore a golden chain about her throat, and was the daughter of King Ethal Anbual. King Ethal's palace was stormed by Ailill, and he was forced to give up his daughter. He gave as a reason for withholding his consent so long, that on Samhain Princess Caer changed from a maiden to a swan, and back again the next year.

"And when the time came Angus went to the loch, and he saw the three times fifty white birds there with their silver chains about their necks, and Angus stood in a man's shape at the edge of the loch, and he called to the girl:
'Come and speak with me, O Caer!'
"'Who is calling me?' said Caer.
"'Angus calls you,' he said, 'and if you do come, I swear by my word I will not hinder you from going into the loch again.'"
—GREGORY: *Cuchulain of Muirthemne.*

She came, and he changed to a swan likewise, and they flew away to King Dagda's palace, where every one who heard their sweet singing was charmed into a sleep of three days and three nights.

Princess Etain, of the race of the Tuatha, and wife of Midir, was born again as the daughter of Queen Medb, the wife of Ailill. She remembers a little of the land from which she came, is never quite happy,

> "But sometimes—sometimes—tell me; have you heard,
>> By dusk or moonset have you ever heard
>> Sweet voices, delicate music? Never seen
>> The passage of the lordly beautiful ones
>> Men call the Shee?"
>> —SHARP: *Immortal Hour*.

even when she wins the love of King Eochaidh. When they have been married a year, there comes Midir from the Land of Youth. By winning a game of chess from the King, he gets anything he may ask, and prays to see the Queen. When he sees her he sings a song of longing to her, and Eochaidh it troubled because it is Samhain, and he knows the great power the hosts of the air "have then over those who wish for happiness."

"Etain, speak!
What is the song the harper sings, what tongue
Is this he speaks? for in no Gaelic lands
Is speech like this upon the lips of men.
No word of all these honey-dripping words
Is known to me. Beware, beware the words
Brewed in the moonshine under ancient oaks
White with pale banners of the mistletoe
Twined round them in their slow and stately death.

It is the feast of Saveen" (Samhain).
    —SHARP: *Immortal Hour.*

In vain Eochaidh pleads with her to stay with him. She had already forgotten all but Midir and the life so long ago in the Land of Youth.

> "In the Land of Youth
> There are pleasant places;
> Green meadows, woods,
> Swift grey-blue waters.
> "There is no age there,
> Nor any sorrow.
> As the stars in heaven
> Are the cattle in the valleys.
> "Great rivers wander
> Through flowery plains.
> Streams of milk, of mead,
> Streams of strong ale.
> "There is no hunger
> And no thirst
> In the Hollow Land,
> In the Land of Youth."
> —SHARP: *Immortal Hour.*

She and Midir fly away in the form of two swans, linked by a chain of gold.

Cuchulain, hopelessly sick of a strange illness brought on by Fand and Liban, fairy sisters, was visited the day before Samhain by a messenger, who promised to cure him if he would go to the Otherworld. Cuchulain could not make up his mind to go, but sent Laeg, his charioteer. Such glorious reports did Laeg bring back from the Otherworld,

"If all Erin were mine,
And the kingship of yellow Bregia,
I would give it, no trifling deed,
To dwell for aye in the place I reached."
—*Cuchulain's Sick-bed.* (Meyer trans.)

that Cuchulain went thither, and
championed the people there against their enemies.
He stayed a month with the fairy Fand. Emer, his
wife at home, was beset with jealousy, and plotted
against Fand, who had follower her hero home.
Fand in fear returned to her deserted husband, Emer
was given a Druidic drink to drown her jealousy,
and Cuchulain another to forget his infatuation, and
they lived happily afterward.

Even after Christianity was made the vital
religion in Ireland, it was believed that places not
exorcised by prayers and by the sign of the cross,
were still haunted by Druids. As late as the fifth
century the Druids kept their skill in fortune-telling.
King Dathi got a Druid to foretell what would
happen to him from one Hallowe'en to the next, and
the prophecy came true. Their religion was now
declared evil, and all evil or at any rate suspicious
beings were assigned to them or to the devil as
followers.

"Maire Bruin:
Are not they, likewise, the children of God?
Father Hart:
Colleen, they are the children of the fiend,
And they have power until the end of Time,
When God shall fight with them a great
pitched battle
And hack them into pieces."

—YEATS: *Land of Heart's Desire.*

The power of fairy music was so great that St. Patrick himself was put to sleep by a minstrel who appeared to him on the day before Samhain. The Tuatha De Danann, angered at the renegade people who no longer did them honor, sent another minstrel, who after laying the ancient religious seat Tara under a twenty-three years' charm, burned up the city with his fiery breath.

These infamous spirits dwelt in grassy mounds, called "forts," which were the entrances to underground palaces full of treasure, where was always music and dancing. These treasure-houses were open only on November Eve

"For the fairy mounds of Erinn are always opened about Hallowe'en."
—*Expedition of Nera.* (Meyer trans.)
when the throngs of spirits, fairies, and goblins trooped out for revels about the country. The old Druid idea of obsession, the besieging of a person by an evil spirit, was practised by them at that time.

"This is the first day of the winter, and to-day the
Hosts of the Air are in their greatest power."
—WARREN: *Twig of Thorn.*

If the fairies wished to seize a mortal— which power they had as the sun-god could take men to himself— they caused him to give them certain tokens by which he delivered himself into their hands. They might be milk and fire—

"Maire Bruin:
A little queer old woman cloaked in green,
Who came to beg a porringer of milk.
Bridget Bruin:
The good people go asking milk and fire
Upon May Eve—woe to the house that gives,
For they have power over it for a year."
    —YEATS: *Land of Heart's Desire.*

    or one might receive a fairy thorn such as
Oonah brings home, which shrivels up at the touch
of St. Bridget's image;

    "Oh, ever since I kept the twig of thorn and
hid it, I have seen strange things, and heard strange
laughter and far voices calling."
    —WARREN: *Twig of Thorn.*

    or one might be lured by music as he
stopped near the fort to watch the dancing, for the
revels were held in secret, as those of the Druids
had been, and no one could look on them
unaffected.
    A story is told of Paddy More, a great stout
uncivil churl, and Paddy Beg, a cheerful little
hunchback. The latter, seeing lights and hearing
music, paused by a mound, and was invited in.
Urged to tell stories, he complied; he danced as
spryly as he could for his deformity; he sang, and
made himself so agreeable that the fairies decided
to take the hump off his back, and send him home a
straight manly fellow. The next Hallowe'en who
should come by the same place but Paddy More,
and he stopped likewise to spy at the merrymaking.
He too was called in, but would not dance politely,

added no stories nor songs. The fairies clapped
Paddy Beg's hump on his back, and dismissed him
under a double burden of discomfort.

A lad called Guleesh, listening outside a fort
on Hallowe'en heard the spirits speaking of the fatal
illness of his betrothed, the daughter of the King of
France. They said that if Guleesh but knew it, he
might boil an herb that grew by his door and give it
to the princess and make her well. Joyfully Guleesh
hastened home, prepared the herb, and cured the
royal girl.

Sometimes people did not have the luck to
return, but were led away to a realm of perpetual
youth and music.

"Father Hart. What are you reading?
Maire Bruin. How a Princess Edane,
A daughter of a King of Ireland, heard
A voice singing on a May Eve like this,
And followed, half awake and half asleep,
Until she came into the land of faery,
Where nobody gets old and godly and grave,
Where nobody gets old and crafty and wise,
Where nobody gets old and bitter of tongue;
And she is still there, busied with a dance,
Deep in the dewy shadow of a wood,
Or where stars walk upon a mountain-top."
—YEATS: *Land of Heart's Desire.*

If one returned, he found that the space
which seemed to him but one night, had been many
years, and with the touch of earthly sod the age he
had postponed suddenly weighed him down.
Ossian, released from fairy land after three hundred
years dalliance there, rode back to his own country

on horseback. He saw men imprisoned under a
block of marble and others trying to lift the stone.
As he leaned over to aid them the girth broke. With
the touch of earth "straightway the white horse fled
away on his way home, the Ossian became aged,
decrepit, and blind."

No place as much as Ireland has kept the
belief in all sorts of supernatural spirits abroad
among its people. From the time when on the hill of
Ward, near Tara, in pre-Christian days, the
sacrifices were burned and the Tuatha were thought
to appear on Samhain, to as late as 1910, testimony
to actual appearances of the :little people" is to be
found.

"'Among the usually invisible races which I
have seen in Ireland, I distinguished five classes.
There are the Gnomes, who are earth-spirits, and
who seem to be a sorrowful race. I once saw some
of them distinctly on the side of Ben Bulbin. They
had rather round heads and dark thick- set bodies,
and in stature were about two and one-half feet. The
Leprechauns are different, being full of mischief,
though they, too, are small. I followed a Leprechaun
from the town of Wicklow out to the Carraig Sidhe,
"Rock of the Fairies," a distance of half a mile or
more, where he disappeared. He had a very merry
face, and beckoned to me with his finger. A third
class are the Little People, who, unlike the Gnomes
and Leprechauns, are quite good-looking; and they
are very small. The Good People are tall, beautiful
beings, as tall as ourselves. . . . They direct the
magnetic currents of the earth. The Gods are really
the Tuatha De Danann, and they are much taller
than our race.'"

—WENTZ: *Fairy-faith in Celtic Countries.*

The sight of the apparitions on Hallowe'en is believed to be fatal to the beholder.

"One night my lady's soul walked along the wall like a cat. Long Tom Bowman beheld her and that day week fell he into the well and was drowned."
—PYLE: *Priest and the Piper.*

One version of the Jack-o'-lantern story comes from Ireland. A stingy man named Jack was for his inhospitality barred from all hope of heaven, and because of practical jokes on the Devil was locked out of hell. Until the Judgement Day he is condemned to walk the earth with a lantern to light his way.

The place of the old lord of the dead, the Tuatha god Saman, to whom vigil was kept and prayers said on November Eve for the good of departed souls, was taken in Christian times by St. Colomba or Columb Kill, the founder of a monastery in Iona in the fifth century. In the seventeenth century the Irish peasants went about begging money and goodies for a feast, and demanding in the name of Columb Kill that fatted calved and black sheep be prepared. In place of the Druid fires, candles were collected and lighted on Hallowe'en, and prayers for the souls of the givers said before them. The name of Saman is kept in the title "Oidhche Shamhna," "vigil of Saman," by which the night of October 31st was until recently called in Ireland.

There are no Hallowe'en bonfires in Ireland

now, but charms and tests are tried. Apples and nuts, the treasure of Pomona, figure largely in these. They are representative winter fruits, the commonest. They can be gathered late and kept all winter.

A popular drink at the Hallowe'en gathering in the eighteenth century was milk in which crushed roasted apples had been mixed. It was called Lambs'-wool (perhaps from "La Mas Ubhal," "the day of the apple fruit"). At the Hallowe'en supper "callcannon," mashed potatoes, parsnips, and chopped onions, is indispensable. A ring is buried in it, and the one who finds it in his portion will be married in a year, or if he is already married, will be lucky.

"They had colcannon, and the funniest things were found in it—tiny dolls, mice, a pig made of china, silver sixpences, a thimble, a ring, and lots of other things. After supper was over all went into the big play-room, and dived for apples in a tub of water, fished for prizes in a basin of flour; then there were games—"
—TRANT: *Hallowe'en in Ireland.*

A coin betokened to the finder wealth; the thimble, that he would never marry.

A ring and a nut are baked in a cake. The ring of course means early marriage, the nut signifies that its finder will marry a widow or widower. If the kernel is withered, no marriage at all is prophesied. In Roscommon, in central Ireland, a coin, a sloe, and a bit of wood were baked in a cake. The one getting the sloe would live longest, the one getting the wood was destined to die within the year.

A mould of flour turned out on the table held similar tokens. Each person cut off a slice with a knife, and drew out his prize with his teeth.

After supper the tests were tried. In the last century nut-shells were burned. The best-known nut test is made as follows: three nuts are named for a girl and two sweethearts. If one burns more steadily with the girl's nut, that love is faithful to her, but if either hers or one of the other nuts starts away, there will be no happy friendship between them.

Apples are snapped from the end of a stick hung parallel to the floor by a twisted cord which whirls the stick rapidly when it is let go. Care has to be taken not to bite the candle burning on the other end. Sometimes this test is made easier by dropping the apples into a tub of water and diving for them, or piercing them with a fork dropped straight down.

Green herbs called "livelong" were plucked by the children and hung up on Midsummer Eve. If a plant was found to be still green on Hallowe'en, the one who had hung it up would prosper for the year, but if it had turned yellow or had died, the child would also die.

Hemp-seed is sown across three furrows, the sower repeating: "Hemp-seed, I saw thee, hemp-seed, I saw thee; and her that is to be my true love, come after me and draw thee." On looking back over his shoulder he will see the apparition of his future wife in the act of gathering hemp.

Seven cabbage stalks were named for any seven of the company, then pulled up, and the guests asked to come out, and "see their sowls."

"One, two, three, and up to seven;

If all are white, all go to heaven;
If one is black as Murtagh's evil,
He'll soon be screechin' wi' the devil."

Red Mike "was a queer one from his birth, an' no wonder, for he first saw the light atween dusk an' dark o' a Hallowe'en Eve." When the cabbage test was tried at a party where Mike was present, six stalks were found to be white, but Mike's was "all black an' fowl wi' worms an' slugs, an' wi' a real bad smell ahint it." Angered at the ridicule he received, he cried: "I've the gift o' the night, I have, an' on this day my curse can blast whatever I choose." At that the priest showed Mike a crucifix, and he ran away howling, and disappeared through a bog into the ground.

—SHARP: *Threefold Chronicle.*

Twelve of the party may learn their future, if one gets a clod of earth from the churchyard, sets up twelve candles in it, lights and names them. The fortune of each will be like that of the candle-light named for him,—steady, wavering, or soon in darkness.

A ball of blue yarn was thrown out of the window by a girl who held fast to the end. She wound it over on her hand from left to right, saying the Creed backwards. When she had nearly finished, she expected the yarn would be held. She must ask "Who holds?" and the wind would sigh her sweetheart's name in at the window.

In some charms the devil was invoked directly. If one walked about a rick nine times with a rake, saying, "I rake this rick in the devil's name," a vision would come and take away the rake.

If one went out with nine grains of oats in

his mouth, and walked about until he heard a girl's name called or mentioned, he would know the name of his future wife, for they would be the same.

Lead is melted, and poured through a key or a ring into cold water. The form each spoonful takes in cooling indicated the occupation of the future husband of the girl who poured it.

"Now something like a horse would cause the jubilant maiden to call out, 'A dragoon!' Now some dim resemblance to a helmet would suggest a handsome member of the mounted police; or a round object with a spike would seem a ship, and this of course meant a sailor; or a cow would suggest a cattle-dealer, or a plough a farmer."
—SHARP: *Threefold Chronicle.*

After the future had been searched, a piper played a jig, to which all danced merrily with a loud noise to scare away the evil spirits.

Just before midnight was the time to go out "alone and unperceived" to a south-running brook, dip a shirt-sleeve in it, bring it home and hang it by the fire to dry. One must go to bed, but watch till midnight for a sight of the destined mate who would come to turn the shirt to dry the other side.

Ashes were raked smooth on the hearth at bedtime on Hallowe'en, and the next morning examined for footprints. If one was turned from the door, guests or a marriage was prophesied; if towards the door, a death.

To have prophetic dreams a girl should search for a briar grown into a hoop, creep through thrice in the name of the devil, cut it in silence, and go to bed with it under her pillow. A boy should cut

ten ivy leaves, throw away one and put the rest
under his head before he slept.

If a girl leave beside her bed a glass of water
with a sliver of wood in it, and say before she falls
asleep:

"Husband mine that is to be,
Come this night and rescue me,"

she will dream of falling off a bridge into
the water, and of being saved at the last minute by
the spirit of her future husband. To receive a drink
from his hand she must eat a cake of flour, soot, and
salt before she goes to bed.

The Celtic spirit of yearning for the
unknown, retained nowhere else as much as in
Ireland, is expressed very beautifully by the poet
Yeats in the introduction to his Celtic Twilight.

"The host is riding from Knocknarea
And over the grave of Clooth-na-bare;
Caolte tossing his burning hair,
And Niam calling: 'away, come away;
"'And brood no more where the fire is
bright,
Filling thy heart with a mortal dream;
For breasts are heaving and eyes a-gleam;
Away, come away to the dim twilight
"'Arms are heaving and lips apart;
And if any gaze on our rushing band,
We come between him and the deed of his
hand,
We come between him and the hope of his
heart.'
"The host is rushing twixt night and day,
And where is there hope or deed as fair?
Caolte tossing his burning hair,

And Niam calling: 'Away, come away.'"

Chapter VIII. In Scotland And The Hebrides

AS in Ireland the Scotch Baal festival of November was called Samhain. Western Scotland, lying nearest Tara, center alike of pagan and Christian religion in Ireland, was colonized by both the people and the customs of eastern Ireland. The November Eve fires which in Ireland either died out of were replaced by candles were continued in Scotland. In Buchan, where was the altar-source of the Samhain fire, bonfires were lighted on hilltops in the eighteenth century; and in Moray the idea of fires of thanksgiving for harvest was kept to as late as 1866. All through the eighteenth century in the Highlands and in Perthshire torches of health, broom, flax, or ferns were carried about the fields and villages by each family, with the intent to cause good crops in succeeding years. The course about the fields was sunwise, to have a good influence. Brought home at dark, the torches were thrown down in a heap, and made a fire. This blaze was called "Samhnagan," "of rest and pleasure." There was much competition to have the largest fire. Each person put in one stone to make a circle about it. The young people ran about with burning brands. Supper was eaten out-of-doors, and games played. After the fire had burned out, ashes were raked over the stones. In the morning each sought his pebble, and if he found it misplaced, harmed, or a footprint marked near it in the ashes, he believed he should die in a year.

In Aberdeenshire boys went about the

villages saying: "Ge's a peat t' burn the witches."
They were thought to be out stealing milk and
harming cattle. Torches used to counteract them
were carried from west to east, against the sun. This
ceremony grew into a game, when a fire was built
by one party, attacked by another, and defended. As
in the May fires of purification the lads lay down in
the smoke close by, or ran about and jumped over
the flames. As the fun grew wilder they flung
burning peats at each other, scattered the ashes with
their feet, and hurried from one fire to another to
have a part in scattering as many as possible before
they died out.

In 1874, at Balmoral, a royal celebration of
Hallowe'en was recorded. Royalty, tenants, and
servants bore torches through the grounds and
round the estates. In front of the castle was a heap
of stuff saved for the occasion. The torches were
thrown on. When the fire was burning its liveliest, a
hobgoblin appeared, drawing in a car the figure of a
witch, surrounded by fairies carrying lances. The
people formed a circle about the fire, and the witch
was tossed in. Then there were dances to the music
of bag-pipes.

It was the time of year when servants
changed masters or signed up anew under the old
ones. They might enjoy a holiday before resuming
work. So they sang:
"This is Hallaeven,
The morn is Halladay;
Nine free nichts till Martinmas,
As soon they'll wear away."

Children born on Hallowe'en could see and
converse with supernatural powers more easily than
others. In Ireland, evil relations caused Red Mike's

downfall (q.v.). For Scotland Mary Avenel, in
Scott's *Monastery,* is the classic example.

"And touching the bairn, it's weel kenn'd she
was born on Hallowe'en, and they that are born on
Hallowe'en whiles see mair than ither folk."

There is no hint of dark relations, but rather
of a clear-sightedness which lays bare truths, even
those concealed in men's breasts. Mary Avenel sees
the spirit of her father after he has been dead for
years. The White Lady of Avenel is her peculiar
guardian.

The Scottish Border, where Mary lived, is
the seat of many superstitions and other worldly
beliefs. The fairies of Scotland are more terrible
than those of Ireland, as the dells and streams and
woods are of greater grandeur, and the character of
the people more serious. It is unlucky to name the
fairies, here as elsewhere, except by such placating
titles as "Good Neighbors" or "Men of Peace."
Rowan, elm, and holly are a protection against
them.

"I have tied red thread round the bairns'
throats, and given ilk ane of them a ride-wand of
rowan-tree, forbye sewing up a slip of witch-elm
into their doublets; and I wish to know of your
reverance if there be onything mair that a lone
woman can do in the matter of ghosts and fairies?—
be here! that I should have named

their unlucky names twice ower!"
—SCOTT: *The Monastery.*

"The sign of the cross disarmeth all evil
spirits."

These spirits of the air have not human

feelings or motives. They are conscienceless. In this respect Peter Pan is an immortal fairy as well as an immortal child. While like a child he resents injustice in horrified silence, like a fairy he acts with no sense of responsibility. When he saves Wendy's brother from falling as they fly,

"You felt it was his cleverness that interested him, and not the saving of human life."
—BARRIE: *Peter and Wendy.*

The world in which Peter lived was so near the Kensington Gardens that he could see them through the bridge as he sat on the shore of Neverland. Yet for a long time he could not get to them.
Peter is a fairy piper who steals away the souls of children.

"No man alive has seen me,
But women hear me play,
Sometimes at door or window,
Fiddling the souls away—
The child's soul and the colleen's
Out of the covering clay."
—HOPPER: *Fairy Fiddler.*
On Hallowe'en all traditional spirits are abroad. The Scotch invented the idea of a "Samhanach," a goblin who comes out just at "Samhain." It is he who in Ireland steals children. The fairies pass at crossroads,

"But the night is Hallowe'en, lady,
The morn is Hallowday;
Then win me, win me, and ye will,

For weel I wot ye may.
"Just at the mirk and midnight hour
The fairy folk will ride.
And they that wad their true-love win,
At Miles Cross they maun bide."
—*Ballad of Tam Lin.*

and in the Highlands whoever took a three-legged stool to where three crossroads met, and sat upon it at midnight, would hear the names of those who were to die in a year. He might bring with him articles of dress, and as each name was pronounced throw one garment to the fairies. They would be so pleased by this gift that they would repeal the sentence of death.

Even people who seemed to be like their neighbors every day could for this night fly away and join the other beings in their revels.

"This is the nicht o' Hallowe'en
When a' the witchie may be seen;
Some o' them black, some o' them green,
Some o' them like a turkey bean."

A witches' party was conducted in this way. The wretched women who had sold their souls to the Devil, left a stick in bed which by evil means was made to have their likeness, and, anointed with the fat of murdered babies flew off up the chimney on a broomstick with cats attendant. Burns tells the story of a company of witches pulling ragwort by the roadside, getting each astride her ragwort with the summons "Up horsie!" and flying away.

"The hag is astride
This night for a ride,
The devils and she together:

Through thick and through thin,
Now out and now in,
Though ne'er so foul be the weather.
* * * * *
"A thorn or a burr
She takes for a spur,
With a lash of the bramble she rides now.
Through brake and through briers,
O'er ditches and mires,
She follows the spirit that guides now."
—HERRICK: *The Hag.*

The meeting-place was arranged by the
Devil, who sometimes rode there on a goat. At their
supper no bread or salt was eaten; they drank out of
horses' skulls, and danced, sometimes back to back,
sometimes from west to east, for the dances at the
ancient Baal festivals were from east to west, and it
was evil and ill-omened to move the other way. For
this dance the Devil played a bag-pipe made of a
hen's skull and cats' tails.

"There sat Auld Nick, in shape o' beast;
A tousie tyke, black, grim, and large,
To gie them music was his charge:
He screw'd the pipes and gart them skirl,
Till roof and rafters a' did dirl [ring]."
—BURNS: *Tam o' Shanter.*

The light for the revelry came from a torch
flaring between the horns of the Devil's steed, the
goat, and at the close the ashes were divided for the
witches to use in incantations. People imagined that
cats who had been up all night on Hallowe'en were
tired out the next morning.

Tam o' Shanter who was watching such a dance
"By Alloway's auld haunted kirk"
in Ayrshire, could not resist calling out at the antics of a neighbor whom he recognized, and was pursued by the witches. He urged his horse to top-speed,

> "Now do thy speedy utmost, Meg,
> And win the key-stane of the brig;
> There at them thou thy tail may toss,
> A running stream they dare na cross!"
> —BURNS: *Tam o' Shanter.*

but poor Meg had no tail thereafter to toss at them, for though she saved her rider, she was only her tail's length beyond the middle of the bridge when the foremost witch grasped it and seared it to a stub.

Such witches might be questioned about the past or future.

> "He that dare sit on St. Swithin's Chair,
> When the Night-Hag wings the troubled air,
> Questions three, when he speaks the spell,
> He may ask, and she must tell."
> —SCOTT: *St. Swithin's Chair.*

Children make of themselves bogies on this evening, carrying the largest turnips they can save from the harvest, hollowed out and carved into the likeness of a fearsome face, with teeth and forehead blacked, and lighted by a candle fastened inside.

If the spirit of a person simply appears without being summoned, and the person is still alive, it means that he is in danger. If he comes toward the one to whom he appears the danger is over. If he seems to go away, he is dying.

An apparition from the future especially is sought on Hallowe'en. It is a famous time for divination in love affairs. A typical eighteenth century party in western Scotland is described by Robert Burns.

Cabbages are important in Scotch superstition. Children believe that if they pile cabbage-stalks round the doors and windows of the house, the fairies will bring them a new brother or sister.

> "And often when in his old-fashioned way
> He questioned me,. . .
> Who made the stars? and if within his hand
> He caught and held one, would his fingers

burn?

> If I, the gray-haired dominie, was dug
> From out a cabbage-garden such as he
> Was found in —"
> —BUCHANAN: *Willie Baird.*

Kale-pulling came first on the program in Burn's Hallowe'en. Just the single and unengaged went out hand in hand blindfolded to the cabbage-garden. They pulled the first stalk they came upon, brought it back to the house, and were unbandaged. The size and shape of the stalk indicated the appearance of the future husband or wife.

"Maybe you would rather not pull a stalk that was tall and straight and strong—that would mean Alastair? Maybe you would rather find you

had got hold of a withered old stump with a lot of earth at the root—a decrepit old man with plenty of money in the bank? Or maybe you are wishing for one that is slim and supple and not so tall—for one that might mean Johnnie Semple."
—BLACK: *Hallowe'en Wraith.*

A close white head meant an old husband, an open green head a young one. His disposition would be like the taste of the stem. To determine his name, the stalks were hung over the door, and the number of one's stalk in the row noted. If Jessie put hers up third from the beginning, and the third man who passed through the doorway under it was named Alan, her husband's first name would be Alan. This is practised only a little now among farmers. It has a special virtue if the cabbage has been stolen from the garden of an unmarried person.

Sometimes the pith of a cabbage-stalk was pushed out, the hole filled with tow, which was set afire and blown through keyholes on Hallowe'en.

"Their runts clean through and through were bored,
And stuffed with raivelins fou,
And like a chimley when on fire
Each could the reek outspue.
"Jock through the key-hole sent a cloud
That reached across the house,
While in below the door reek rushed
Like water through a sluice."
—DICK: *Splores of a Hallowe'en.*

Cabbage-broth was a regular dish at the Hallowe'en feast. Mashed potatoes, as in Ireland, or

a dish of meal and milk holds symbolic objects—a
ring, a thimble, and a coin. In the cake are baked a
ring and a key. The ring signifies to the possessor
marriage, and the key a journey.

Apple-ducking is still a universal custom in
Scotland. A sixpence is sometimes dropped into the
tub or stuck into an apple to make the reward
greater. The contestants must keep their hands
behind their backs.

Nuts are put before the fire in pairs, instead
of by threes as in Ireland, and named for a lover and
his lass. If they burn to ashes together, a long happy
married life is destined to the lovers. If they crackle
or start away from each other, dissension and
separation are ahead.

> "Jean slips in twa, wi' tentie [careful] e'e;
> Wha 't was, she wadna tell;
> But this is Jack, an' this is me,
> She says in to hersel;
> He bleez'd owre her, an' she owre him,
> As they wad never mair part;
> Till fuff! he started up the lum [chimney],
> And Jean had e'en a sair heart
> To see't that night."
> —BURNS: *Hallowe'en.*

Three "luggies," bowls with handles like the
Druid lamps, were filled, one with clean, one with
dirty water, and one left empty. The person wishing
to know his fate in marriage was blindfolded, turned
about thrice, and put down his left hand. If he
dipped it into the clean water, he would marry a
maiden; if into the dirty, a widow; if into the empty
dish, not at all. He tried until he got the same result
twice. The dishes were changed about each time.

This spell still remains, as does that of hemp-seed sowing. One goes out alone with a handful of hemp-seed, sows it across ridges of ploughed land, and harrows it with anything convenient, perhaps with a broom. Having said:

> "Hemp-seed, I saw thee,
> An' her that is to be my lass
> Come after me an' draw thee—"
> —BURNS: *Hallowe'en.*

he looks behind him to see his sweetheart gathering hemp. This should be tried just at midnight with the moon behind.

> "At even o' Hallowmas no sleep I sought,
> But to the field a bag of hemp-seed brought.
> I scattered round the seed on every side,
> And three times three in trembling accents cried,
> 'This hemp-seed with my virgin hand I sow,
> Who shall my true-love be, the crop shall mow'"
> —GAY: *Pastorals.*

A spell that has been discontinued is throwing the clue of blue yarn into the kiln-pot, instead of out of the window, as in Ireland. As it is wound backward, something holds it. The winder must ask, "Wha hauds?" to hear the name of her future sweetheart.

> "An' ay she win't, an' ay she swat—
> I wat she made nae jaukin;
> Till something held within the pat,

Guid Lord! but she was quakin!
But whether 't was the Deil himsel,
Or whether 't was a bauk-en' [cross-beam]
Or whether it was Andrew Bell,
She did na wait on talkin
To speir [ask] that night."
—BURNS: *Hallowe'en.*

Another spell not commonly tried now is winnowing three measures of imaginary corn, as one stands in the barn alone with both doors open to let the spirits that come in go out again freely. As one finishes the motions, the apparition of the future husband will come in at one door and pass out at the other.

"'I had not winnowed the last weight clean out, and the moon was shining bright upon the floor, when in stalked the presence of my dear Simon Glendinning, that is now happy. I never saw him plainer in my life than I did that moment; he held up an arrow as he passed me, and I swarf'd awa' wi' fright. . . . But mark the end o' 't, Tibb: we were married, and the grey-goose wing was the death o' him after a'.'"
—SCOTT: *The Monastery.*

At times other prophetic appearances were seen.

"Just as she was at the wark, what does she see in the moonlicht but her ain coffin moving between the doors instead of the likeness of a gudeman! and as sure's death she was in her coffin before the same time next year."

—ANON: *A Tale of Hallowe'en.*

Formerly a stack of beans, oats, or barley was measured round with the arms against the sun. At the end of the third time the arms would enclose the vision of the future husband or wife.

Kale-pulling, apple-snapping, and lead-melting (see Ireland) are social rites, but many were to be tried alone and in secret. A highland divination was tried with a shoe, held by the tip, and thrown over the house. The person will journey in the direction the toe points out. If it falls sole up, it means bad luck.

Girls would pull a straw each out of a thatch in Broadsea, and would take it to an old woman in Fraserburgh. The seeress would break the straw and find within it a hair the color of the lover's-to-be. Blindfolded they plucked heads of oats, and counted the number of grains to find out how many children they would have. If the tip was perfect, not broken or gone, they would be married honorably.

Another way of determining the number of children was to drop the white of an egg into a glass of water. The number of divisions was the number sought. White of egg is held with water in the mouth, like the grains of oats in Ireland, while one takes a walk to hear mentioned the name of his future wife. Names are written on papers and laid upon the chimney-piece. Fate guides the hand of a blindfolded man to the slip which bears his sweetheart's name.

A Hallowe'en mirror is made by the rays of the moon shining into a looking-glass. If a girl goes secretly into a room at midnight between October and November, sits down at the mirror, and cuts an apple into nine slices, holding each on the point of a knife before she eats it, she may see in the moonlit glass the image of her lover looking over her left shoulder, and asking for the last piece of apple.

The wetting of the sark-sleeve in a south-running burn where "three lairds' lands meet," and carrying it home to dry before the fire, was really a Scotch custom, but has already been described in Ireland.

"The last Hallowe'en I was waukin
[watching]
My droukit [drenched] sark-sleeve, as ye
kin—
His likeness came up the house staukin,
And the very grey breeks o' Tam Glen!"
—BURNS: *Tam Glen.*

Just before breaking up, the crowd of young people partook of sowens, oatmeal porridge cakes with butter, and strunt, a liquor, as they hoped for good luck throughout the year.

The Hebrides, Scottish islands off the western coast, have Hallowe'en traditions of their own, as well as many borrowed from Ireland and Scotland. Barra, isolated near the end of the island chain, still celebrates the Celtic days, Beltaine and November Eve. In the Hebrides is the Irish custom of eating on Hallowe'en a cake of meal and salt, or a salt herring, bones and all, to dream of some one bringing a drink of water. Not a word must be spoken, nor a drop of water drunk till the dream comes.

In St. Kilda a large triangular cake is baked which must be all eaten up before morning.

A curious custom that prevailed in the island of Lewis in the eighteenth century was the worhip of Shony, a sea-god with a Norse name. His ceremonies were similar to those paid to Saman in Ireland, but more picturesque. Ale was brewed at church from malt brought collectively by the people. One took a cupful in his hand, and waded out into the sea up to his waist, saying as he poured it out: "Shony, I give you this cup of ale, hoping that you'll be so kind as to send us plenty of sea-ware, for enriching our ground the ensuing year." The party returned to the church, waited for a given signal when a candle burning on the altar was blown out. Then they went out into the fields, and drank ale with dance and song.

The "dumb cake" originated in Lewis. Girls were each apportioned a small piece of dough, mixed with any but spring water. They kneaded it with their left thumbs, in silence. Before midnight they pricked initials on them with a new pin, and put them by the fire to bake. The girls withdrew to the farther end of the room, still in silence. At midnight each lover was expected to enter and lay his hand on the cake marked with his initials.

In South Uist and Eriskay on Hallowe'en fairies are out, a source of terror to those they meet.

"Hallowe'en will come, will come,
Witchcraft will be set a-going,
Fairies will be at full speed,
Running in every pass.
Avoid the road, children, children."

But for the most part this belief has died out on Scottish land, except near the Border, and Hallowe'en is celebrated only by stories and jokes and games, songs and dances.

Chapter IX. In England and Man

MAN especially has a treasury of fairy tradition, Celtic and Norse combined. Manx fairies too dwell in the middle world, since they are fit for neither heaven nor hell. Even now Manx people think they see circles of light in the late October midnight, and little folk dancing within.   Longest of all in Man was Sauin (Samhain) considered New Year's Day. According to the old style of reckoning time it came on November 12.

"To-night is New Year's night.
Hogunnaa!"
—*Mummers' Song.*

As in Scotland the servants' year end with October.

New Year tests for finding out the future were tried on Sauin. To hear her sweetheart's name a girl took a mouthful of water and two handfuls of salt, and sat down at a door. The first name she heard mentioned was the wished-for one. The three dishes proclaimed the fate of the blindfolded seeker as in Scotland. Each was blindfolded and touched one of several significant objects—meal for prosperity, earth for death, a net for tangled fortunes.

Before retiring each filled a thimble with salt, and emptied it out in a little mound on a plate, remembering his own. If any heap were found fallen over by morning, the person it represented was destined to die in a year. The Manx looked for prints in the smooth-strewn ashes on the hearth, as the Scotch did, and gave the same interpretation.

There had been Christian churches in Britain as early as 300 A.D., and Christian missionaries, St. Ninian, Pelagius, and St. Patrick, were active in the next century, and in the course of time St. Augustine. Still the old superstitions persisted, as they always do when they have grown up with the people.

King Arthur, who was believed to have reigned in the fifth century, may be a personification of the sun-god. He comes from the Otherworld, his magic sword Excalibur is brought thence to him, he fights twelve battles in number like the months, and is wounded to death by evil Modred, once his own knight. He passes in a boat, attended by his fairy sister and two other queens,

> "'To the island-valley of Avilion;
> Where falls not hail, or rain, or any snow,
> Nor ever wind blows loudly; but it lies
> Deep-meadowed, happy, fair with orchard-

lawns

> And bowery hollows crown'd with summer

sea—'"

—TENNYSON: *Passing of Arthur.*

The hope of being healed there is like that given to Cuchulain (q.v.), to persuade him to visit the fairy kingdom. Arthur was expected to come again sometime, as the sun renews his course. As he disappeared from the sight of Bedivere, the last of his knights,

> "The new sun rose bringing the new year."

—*Ibid.*

Avilion means "apple-island." It was like the Heperides of Greek mythology, the western islands where grew the golden apples of immortality.

In Cornwall after the sixth century, the sun-god became St. Michael, and the eastern point where he appeared St. Michael's seat.

"Where the great vision of the guarded mount

Looks toward Namancos, and Bayona's hold."

—MILTON: *Lycidas.*

As fruit to Pomona, so berries were devoted to fairies. They would not let any one cut a blackthorn shoot on Hallowe'en. In Cornwall sloes and blackberries were considered unfit to eat after the fairies had passed by, because all the goodness was extracted. So they were eaten to heart's content on October 31st, and avoided thereafter. Hazels, because they were thought to contain wisdom and knowledge, were also sacred.

Besides leaving berries for the "Little People," food was set out for them on Hallowe'en, and on other occasions. They rewarded this hospitality by doing an extra-ordinary amount of work.

"—how the drudging goblin sweat
To earn his cream-bowl duly set,
When in one night, ere glimpse of morn,
His shadowy flail hath threshed the corn
That ten day-laborers could not end.
Then lies him down the lubbar fiend,
And strecht out all the chimney's length
Basks at the fire his hairy strength."
—MILTON: *L'Allegro.*

Such sprites did not scruple to pull away the

chair as one was about to sit down, to pinch, or even to steal children and leave changelings in their places. The first hint of dawn drove them back to their haunts.

> "When larks 'gin sing,
> Away we fling;
> And babes new borne steal as we go,
> And elfe in bed
> We leave instead,
> And wend us laughing, ho, ho, ho!"
> —JONSON: *Robin Goodfellow.*

Soulless and without gratitude or memory spirits of the air may be, like Ariel in The Tempest. He, like the fairy harpers of Ireland, puts men to sleep with his music.

> "Sebastian. What, art thou waking?
> Antonio. Do you not hear me speak?
> Sebastian: I do; and surely,
> It is a sleepy language; and thou speak'st
> Out of thy sleep: What is it thou didst say?
> This is a strange repose, to be asleep
> With eyes wide open; standing, speaking, moving,
> And yet so fast asleep."
> —SHAKESPEARE: *The Tempest.*

The people of England, in common with those who lived in other countries of Great Britain and in Europe, dreaded the coming of winter not only on account of the cold and loneliness, but because they believed that at this time the powers of evil were abroad and ascendant. This belief harked back to the old idea that the sun had been vanquished by his enemies in the late autumn. It was to forget the fearful influences about them that the English kept festival so much in the winter-time. The Lords of Misrule, leaders of the revelry, "beginning their rule on All Hallow Eve, continued the same till the morrow after the Feast of the Purification, commonlie called Candlemas day: In all of which space there were fine and sublte disguisinges, Maskes, and Mummeries." This was written of King Henry IV's court at Eltham, in 1401, and is true of centuries before and after. They gathered about the fire and made merry while the October tempests whirled the leaves outsidem and shrieked round the house like ghosts and demons on a mad carousal.

> "The autumn wind—oh hear it howl:
> Without—October's tempests scowl,
> As he troops away on the raving wind!
> And leaveth dry leaves in his path behind.
> * * * * *
> "'T is the night—the night
> Of the graves' delightm
> And the warlock [devils] are at their play!
> Ye think that without
> The wild winds shout,
> But no, it is they—it is they!"
> —COXE: *Hallowe'en.*

Witchcraft—the origin of which will be traced farther on—had a strong following in England. The three witches in Macbeth are really fates who foretell the future, but they have a kettle in which they boil

"Fillet of a fenny snake,
* * * * *
Eye of newt, and toe of frog,
Wool of bat, and tongue of dog,
Adder's fork, and blindworm's sting,
Lizard's leg, and owlet's wing,
For a charm of powerful trouble—"
—SHAKESPEARE: *Macbeth*

They connect themselves thereby with those evil creatures who pursued Tam o'Shanter, and were servants of the Devil. In 1892 in Lincolnshire, people believed that if they looked in through the church door on Hallowe'en they would see the Devil preaching his doctrines from the pulpit, and inscribing the names of new witches in his book.

The Spectre Huntman, known in Windsor Forest as Herne the Hunter, and in Todmorden as Gabriel Ratchets, was the spirit of an ungodly hunter who for his crimes was condemned to lead the chase till Judgement Day. In a storm on Hallowe'en is heard the belling of his hounds.

"Still, still shall last the dreadful chase
Till time itself shall have an end;
By day they scour earth's cavern'd space,
At midnight's witching hour, ascend.
"This is the horn, the hound, and horse,
That oft the lated peasant hears:
Appall'd, he signs the frequent cross,
When the wild din invades his ears."
—SCOTT: *Wild Huntsman.*

In the north of England Hallowe'en was called "nut-crack" and "snap-apple night." It was celebrated by "young people and sweethearts."

A variation of the nut test is, naming two for four lovers before they are put before the fire to roast. The unfaithful lover's nut cracks and jumps away, the loyal burns with a steady ardent flame to ashes.

> "Two hazel-nuts I threw into the flame,
> And to each nut I gave a sweetheart's name.
> This with the loudest bounce me sore
amaz'd,
> That in a flame of brightest color blaz'd;
> As blaz'd the nut, so may thy passion grow,
> For 't was thy nut that did so brightly glow."
> —GAY: *The Spell.*

If they jump toward each other, they will be rivals. If one of the nuts has been named for the girl and burns quietly with a lover's nut, they will live happily together. If they are restless, there is trouble ahead.

> "These glowing nuts are emblems true
> Of what in human life we view;
> The ill-matched couple fret and fume,
> And thus in strife themselves consume,
> Or from each other wildly start
> And with a noise forever part.
> But see the happy, happy pair
> Of genuine love and truth sincere;
> With mutual fondness, while they burn
> Still to each other kindly turn:
> And as the vital sparks decay,
> Together gently sink away.
> Till, life's fierce ordeal being past,

Their mingled ashes rest at last."
—GRAYDON: *On Nuts Burning,
Allhallows Eve.*

Sometimes peas on a hot shovel are used instead.

Down the centuries from the Druid tree-worship comes the spell of the walnut-tree. It is circled thrice, with the invocation: "Let her that is to be my true-love bring me some walnuts;" and directly a spirit will be seen in the tree gathering nuts.

"Last Hallow Eve I sought a walnut-tree,
In hope my true Love's face that I might see;
Three times I called, three times I walked apace;
Then in the tree I saw my true Love's face."
—GAY: *Pastorals.*

The seeds of apples were used in many trials. Two stuck on cheeks or eyelids indicated by the time they clung the faithfulness of the friends named for them.

"See, from the core two kernels brown I take:
This on my cheek for Lubberkin is worn,
And Booby Clod on t'other side is borne;
But Booby Clod soon drops upon the ground,
A certain token that his love's unsound;
While Lubberkin sticks firmly to the last.
Oh! were his lips to mine but joined so fast."
—GAY: *Pastorals.*

In a tub float stemless apples, to be seized by the teeth of him desirous of having his love returned. If he is successful in bringing up the apple, his love-affair will end happily.

"The rosy apple's bobbing
Upon the mimic sea—
'T is tricksy and elusive,
And glides away from me.
"One moment it is dreaming
Beneath the candle's glare,
Then over wave and eddy
It glances here and there.
"And when at last I capture
The prize with joy aglow,
I sigh, may I this sunshine
Of golden rapture know
"When I essay to gether
In all her witchery
Love's sweetest rosy apple
On Love's uncertain sea."
—MUNKITTRICK: *Hallowe'en Wish.*

An apple is peeled all in one piece, and the paring swung three times round the head and dropped behind the left shoulder. If it does not break, and is looked at over the shoulder it forms the initial of the true sweetheart's name.

"I pare this pippin round and round again,
My sweetheart's name to flourish on the
plain:
I fling the unbroken paring o'er my head.
A perfect 'L' upon the ground is read."

—GAY: *Pastorals.*

In the north of England was a unique custom, "the scadding of peas." A pea-pod was slit, a bean pushed inside, and the opening closed again. The full pods were boiled, and apportioned to be shelled and the peas eaten with butter and salt. The one finding the bean on his plate would be married first.

Gay records another test with peas which is like the final trial made with kale-stalks.

"As peascods once I plucked I chanced to see
One that was closely filled with three times three;
Which when I crop'd, I safely home convey'd,
And o'er the door the spell in secret laid;—
The latch moved up, when who should first come in,
But in his proper person—Lubberkin."
—GAY: *Pastorals.*

Candles, relics of the sacred fire, play an important part everywhere on Hallowe'en. In England too the lighted candle and the apple were fastened to the stick, and as it whirled, each person in turn sprang up and tried to bite the apple.

"Or catch th' elusive apple with a bound,
As with the taper it flew whizzing round."

This was a rough game, more suited to boys' frolic than the ghostly divinations that preceded it. Those with energy to spare found material to exercise it on. In an old book there is a picture of a youth sitting on a stick placed across two stools. On one end of the stick is a lighted candle from which he is trying to light another in his hand. Beneath is a tub of water to receive him if he over-balances sideways. These games grew later into practical jokes.

The use of a goblet may perhaps come from the story of "The Luck of Edenhall," a glass stolen from the fairies, and holding ruin for the House by whom it was stolen, if it should ever be broken. With ring and goblet this charm was tried: the ring, symbol of marriage, was suspended by a hair within a glass, and a name spelled out by beginning the alphabet over each time the ring struck the glass.

When tired of activity and noise, the party gathered about a story-teller, or passed a bundle of fagots from hand to hand, each selecting one and reciting an installment of the tale till his stick burned to ashes.

"I tell ye the story this chill Hallowe'en,
For it suiteth the spirit-eve."
—COXE: *Hallowe'en.*

To induce prophetic dreams the wood-and-water test was tried in England also.

"Last Hallow Eve I looked my love to see,
And tried a spell to call her up to me.
With wood and water standing by my side
I dreamed a dream, and saw my own sweet bride."

Though Hallowe'en is decidedly a country festival, in the seventeenth century young gentlemen in London chose a Master of the Revels, and held masques and dances with their friends on this night.

In central and southern England the

ecclesiastical side of Hallowtide is stressed.

Bread or cake has till recently (1898) been as much a part of Hallowe'en preparations as plum pudding at Christmas. Probably this originated from an autumn baking of bread from the new grain. In Yorkshire each person gets a triangular seed-cake, and the evening is called "cake night."

"Wife, some time this weeke, if the wether hold cleere,
An end of wheat-sowing we make for this yeare.
Remember you, therefore, though I do it not,
The seed-cake, the Pasties, and Furmentie-pot."
—TUSSER: *Five Hundred Points of Good Husbandry,* 1580

Cakes appear also at the vigil of All Souls', the next day. At a gathering they lie in a heap for the guests to take. In return they are supposed to say prayers for the dead.

"A Soule-cake, a Soule-cake; have mercy on all Christen souls for a Soule-cake."
—*Old Saying.* The poor in Staffordshire and Shropshire went about singing for soul-cakes or money, promising to pray and to spend the alms in masses for the dead. The cakes were called Soul-mass or "somas" cakes.

"Soul! Soul! for a soul-cake;
Pray, good mistress, for a soul-cake.
One for Peter, two for Paul,
Three for them who made us all."
—*Notes and Queries.*

In Dorsetshire Hallowe'en was celebrated by the ringing of bells in memory of the dead. King Henry VIII and later Queen Elizabeth issued commands against this practice.

In Lancashire in the early nineteenth century people used to go about begging for candles to drive away the gatherings of witches. If the lights were kept burning till midnight, no evil influence could remain near.

In Derbyshire, central England, torches of straw were carried about the stacks on All Souls' Eve, not to drive away evil spirits, as in Scotland, but to light souls through Purgatory.

Like the Bretons, the English have the superstition that the dead return on Hallowe'en.

> '"Why do you wait at your door, woman,
> Alone in the night?'
> 'I am waiting for one who will come,
> stranger,
> To show him a light.
> He will see me afar on the road,
> And be glad at the sight.'
> '"Have you no fear in your heart, woman,
> To stand there alone?
> There is comfort for you and kindly content
> Beside the hearthstone.'
> But she answered, 'No rest can I have
> Till I welcome my own.'
> '"Is it far he must travel to-night,
> This man of your heart?'
> 'Strange lands that I know not, and pitiless
> seas
> Have kept us apart,

And he travels this night to his home
Without guide, without chart.'
'"And has he companions to cheer him?'
'Aye, many,' she said.
'The candles are lighted, the hearthstones are
swept,
The fires glow red.
We shall welcome them out of the night—
Our home-coming dead.'"
—LETTES: *Hallowe'en.*

Chapter X. In Wales

IN Wales the custom of fires persisted from the time of the Druid festival-days longer than in any other place. First sacrifices were burned, the creatures merely passed through the fire; and with the rise of Christianity fire was thought to be a protection against the evil power of the same gods. Pontypridd, in South Wales, was the Druid religious center of Wales. It is still marked by a stone circle and an altar on a hill. In after years it was believed that the stones were people changed to that form by the power of a witch.

In North Wales the November Eve fire, which each family built in the most prominent place near the house, was called Coel Coeth. Into the dying fire each member of the family threw a white stone marked so that he could recognize it again. Circling about the fire hand-in-hand they said their prayers and went to bed. In the morning each searched for his stone, and if he could not find it, he believed that he would die within the next twelve months. This is still credited. There is now the custom also of watching the fires till the last spark dies, and instantly rushing down the hill, "the devil (or the cutty black sow) take the hindmost." A Cardiganshire proverb says:

"A cutty [short-tailed] black sow
On every stile,
Spinning and carding
Every Allhallows' Eve."

November Eve was called "Nos-Galan-Gaeof," the night of the winter Calends, that is, the night before the first day of winter. To the Welsh it was New Year's Eve.

Welsh fairy tradition resembles that in the near-by countries. There is an old story of a man who lay down to sleep inside a fairy ring, a circle of greener grass where the fairies danced by night. The fairies carried him away and kept him seven years, and after he had been rescued from them he would neither eat nor speak.

In the sea was the Otherworld, a
"Green fairy island reposing
In sunlight and beauty on ocean's calm breast."
—PARRY: *Welsh Melodies.*

This was the abode of the Druids, and hence of all supernatural beings, who were
"Something betwixt heaven and hell,
Something that neither stood nor fell."
—SCOTT: *The Monastery.*

As in other countries the fairies or pixies are to be met at crossroads, where happenings, such as funerals, may be witnessed weeks before they really occur.

At the Hallow Eve supper parsnips and cakes are eaten, and nuts and apples roasted. A "puzzling jug" holds the ale. In the rim are three holes that seem merely ornamental. They are connected with the bottom of the jug by pipes through the handle, and the unwitting toper is well drenched unless he is clever enough to see that he must stop up two of the holes, and drink through the third.

Spells are tried in Wales too with apples and nuts. There is dicking and snapping for apples. Nuts are thrown into the fire, denoting prosperity if they blaze brightly, misfortune if they pop, or smoulder and turn black.

"Old Pally threw on a nut. It flickered and then blazed up. Maggee tossed one into the fire. It smouldered and gave no light."

-MARKS: *All-Hallows Honeymoon.*

Fate is revealed by the three luggies and the ball of yarn thrown out of the window: Scotch and Irish charms. The leek takes the place of the cabbage in Scotland. Since King Cadwallo decorated his soldiers with leeks for their valor in a battle by a leek-garden, they have been held in high esteem in Wales. A girl sticks a knife among leeks at Hallowe'en, and walks backward out of the garden. She returns later to find that her future husband has picked up the knife and thrown it into the center of the leek-bed.

Taking two long-stemmed roses, a girl goes to her room in silence. She twines the stems together, naming one for her sweetheart and the other for herself, and thinking this rhyme:

"Twine, twine, and intertwine.
Let his love be wholly mine.
If his heart be kind and true,
Deeper grow his rose's hue."

She can see, by watching closely, her lover's rose grow darker.

The sacred ash figures in one charm. The party of young people seek an even-leaved sprig of ash. The first who finds one calls out "cyniver." If a boy calls out first, the first girl who finds another perfect shoot bears the name of the boy's future wife.

Dancing and singing to the music of the harp close the evening.

Instead of leaving stones in the fire to determine who are to die, people now go to church to be by the light of a candle held in the hand the spirits of those who will not be alive next Hallowe'en.

On the Eve of All Souls' Day, twenty-four hours after Hallowe'en, children in eastern Wales go from house to house singing for

"An apple or a pear, a plum or a cherry,
Or any good thing to make us merry."

It is a time when charity is given freely to the poor. On this night and the next day, fires are burned, as in England, to light souls through Purgatory, and prayers are made for a good wheat harvest next year by the Welsh, who keep the forms of religion very devoutly.

Chapter XI. In Brittany and France

THE Celts had been taught by their priests that the soul is immortal. When the body died the spirit passed instantly into another existence in a country close at hand. We remember that the Otherworld of the British Isles, peopled by the banished Tuatha and all superhuman beings, was either in caves in the earth, as in Ireland, or in an island like the English Avalon. By giving a mortal one of their magic apples to eat, fairies could entice him whither they would, and at last away into their country. In the Irish story of Nera (q.v.), the corpse of the criminal is the cause of Nera's being lured into the cave. So the dead have the same power as fairies, and live in the same place. On May Eve and November Eve the dead and the fairies hold their revels together and make excursions together. If a young person died, he was said to be called away by the fairies. The Tuatha may not have been a race of gods, but merely the early Celts, who grew to godlike proportions as the years raised a mound of lore and legends for their pedestal. So they might really be only the dead, and not of superhuman nature.

In the fourth century A.D., the men of England were hard pressed by the Picts and Scots from the northern border, and were helped in their need by the Teutons. When this tribe saw the fair country of the Britons they decided to hold it for themselves. After they had driven out the northern tribes, in the fifth century, when King Arthur was reigning in Cornwall, they drove out those whose

cause they had fought. So the Britons were scattered
to the mountains of Wales, to Cornwall, and across
the Channel to Armorica, a part of France, which
they named Brittany after their home-land. In lower
Brittany, out of the zone of French influence, a
language something like Welsh or old British is still
spoken, and many of the Celtic beliefs were
retained more untouched than in Britain, not clear
of paganism till the seventeenth century. Here
especially did Christianity have to adapt the old
belief to her own ends.

Gaul, as we have seen from Caesar's
account, had been one of the chief seats of
Druidical belief. The religious center was Carnutes,
now Chartrain. The rites of sacrifice survived in the
same forms as in the British Isles. In the fields of
Deux-Sevres fires were built of stubble, ferns,
leaves, and thorns, and the people danced about
them and burned nuts in them. On St. John's Day
animals were burned in the fires to secure the cattle
from disease. This was continued down into the
seventeenth century.

The pagan belief that lasted the longest in
Brittany, and is by no means dead yet, was the cult
of the dead. Caesar said that the Celts of Gaul
traced their ancestry from the god of death, whom
he called Dispater. Now figures of l'Ankou, a
skeleton armed with a spear, can be seen in most
villages of Brittany.

This mindfulness of death was strengthened
by the sight of the prehistoric cairns of stones on
hilltops, the ancient altars of the Druids, and
dolmens, formed of one flat rock resting like a roof
on two others set up on end with a space between
them, ancient tombs; and by the Bretons being cut

off from the rest of France by the nature of the country, and shut in among the uplands, black and misty in November, and blown over by chill Atlantic winds. Under a seeming dull indifference and melancholy the Bretons conceal a lively imagination, and no place has a greater wealth of legendary literature.

What fairies, dwarfs, pixies, and the like are to the Celts of other places, the spirits of the dead are to the Celts of Brittany. They possess the earth on Christmas, St. John's Day, and All Saints'. In Finistere, that western point of France, there is a saying that on the Eve of All Souls' "There are more dead in every house than sands on the shore." The dead have the power to charm mortals and take them away, and to foretell the future. They must not be spoken of directly, any more than the fairies of the Scottish border, or met with, for fear of evil results.

By the Bretons of the sixth century the near-by island of Britain, which they could just see on clear days, was called the Otherworld. An historian, Procopius, tells how the people nearest Britain were exempted from paying tribute to the Franks, because they were subject to nightly summons to ferry the souls of the dead across in their boats, and deliver them into the hands of the keeper of souls. Farther inland a black bog seemed to be the entrance to an otherworld underground. One location which combined the ideas of an island and a cave was a city buried in the sea. The people imagined they could hear the bells of Ker-Is ringing, and joyous music sounding, for though this was a city of the dead, it resembled the fairy palaces of Ireland, and was ruled by King Grallon and his daughter Dahut, who could lure mortals away by her beauty and enchantments.

The approach of winter is believed to drive like the flocks, the souls of the dead from their cold cheerless graves to the food and warmth of home. This is why November Eve, the night before the first day of winter, was made sacred to them.

"When comes the harvest of the year
Before the scythe the wheat will fall."
—BOTREL: *Songs of Brittany.*

The harvest-time reminded the Bretons of the garnering by that reaper, Death. On November Eve milk is poured on graves, feasts and candles set out on the tables, and fires lighted on the hearths to welcome the spirits of departed kinsfolk and friends.

In France from the twelfth to the fourteenth century stone buildings like lighthouses were erected in cemeteries. They were twenty or thirty feet high, with lanterns on top. On Hallowe'en they were kept burning to safe-guard the people from the fear of night-wandering spirits and the dead, so they were called "lanternes des morts."

The cemetery is the social center of the Breton village. It is at once meeting-place, playground, park, and church. The tombs that outline the hills make the place seem one vast cemetery. On All Souls' Eve in the mid-nineteenth century the "procession of tombs" was held. All formed a line and walked about the cemetery, calling the names of those who were dead, as they approached their resting-places. The record was carefully remembered, so that not one should seem to be forgotten.

"We live with our dead," Say the Bretons.

First on the Eve of All Souls' comes the religious service, "black vespers." The blessedness of death is praised, the sorrows and shortness of life dwelt upon. After a common prayer all go out to the cemetery to pray separately, each by the graves of his kin, or to the "place of bones," where the remains of those long dead are thrown all together in one tomb. They can be seen behind gratings, by the people as they pass, and rows of skulls at the sides of the entrance can be touched.

In these tombs are Latin inscriptions meaning: "Remember thou must die," "To-day to me, and to-morrow to thee," and others reminding the reader of his coming death.

From the cemetery the people go to a house or an inn which is the gathering-place for the night, singing or taking loudly on the road to warn the dead who are hastening home, lest they may meet. Reunions of families take place on this night, in the spirit of the Roman feast of the dead, the Feralia, of which Ovid wrote:

"After the visit to the tombs and to the ancestors who are no longer with us, it is pleasant to turn towards the living; after the loss of so many, it is pleasant to behold those who remain of our blood, and to reckon up the generations of our descendants."
—*Fasti.*

A toast is drunk to the memory of the departed. The men sit about the fireplace smoking or weaving baskets; the women apart, knitting or spinning by the light of the fire and one candle. The children play with their gifts of apples and nuts. As the hour grows later, and mysterious noises begin to be heard about the house, and a curtain sways in a draught, the thoughts of the company already centred upon the dead find expression in words, and each has a tale to tell of an adventure with some friend or enemy who has died.

The dead are thought to take up existence where they left it off, working at the same trades, remembering their old debts, likes and dislikes, even wearing the same clothes they wore in life. Most of them stay not in some distant, definite Otherworld, but frequent the scenes of their former life. They never trespass upon daylight, and it is dangerous to meet them at night, because they are very ready to punish any slight to their memory, such as selling their possessions or forgetting the hospitality due them. L'Ankou will come to get a supply of shavings if the coffins are not lined with them to make a softer resting-place for the dead bodies.

The lively Celtic imagination turns the merest coincidence into an encounter with a spirit, and the poetic temperament of the narrators clothes the stories with vividness and mystery. They tell how the presence of a ghost made the midsummer air so cold that even wood did not burn, and of groans and footsteps underground as long as the ghost is displeased with what his relatives are doing.

Just before midnight a bell-man goes about the streets to give warning of the hour when the spirits will arrive.

"They will sit where we sat, and will talk of us as we talked of them: in the gray of the morning

only will they go away."
—LE BRAZ: *Night of the Dead.*

The supper for the souls is then set out. The poor who live on the mountains have only black corn, milk, and smoked bacon to offer, but it is given freely. Those who can afford it spread on a white cloth dishes of clotted milk, hot pancakes, and mugs of cider.

After all have retired to lie with both eyes shut tight lest they see one of the guests, death-singers make their rounds, chanting under the windows:

"You are comfortably lying in your bed,
But with the poor dead it is otherwise;
You are stretched softly in your bed
While the poor souls are wandering abroad.
"A white sheet and five planks,
A bundle of straw beneath the head,
Five feet of earth above
Are all the worldly goods we own."
—LE BRAZ: *Night of the Dead.*

The tears of their deserted friends disturb the comfort of the dead, and sometimes they appear to tell those in sorrow that their shrouds are always wet from the tears shed on their graves.

Wakened by the dirge of the death-singers the people rise and pray for the souls of the departed.

Divination has little part in the annals of the evening, but one in Finistere is recorded. Twenty-five new needles are laid in a dish, and named, and water is poured upon them. Those who cross are enemies.

In France is held a typical Continental celebration of All Saints' and All Souls'. On October 31st the children go asking for flowers to decorate the graves, and to adorn the church. At night bells ring to usher in All Saints'. On the day itself the churches are decorated gaily with flowers, candles, and banners, and a special service is held. On the second day of November the light and color give way to black drapings, funeral songs, and prayers.

Chapter XII. The Teutonic Religion. Witches

THE Teutons, that race of northern peoples called by the Romans, "barbarians," comprised the Goths and Vandals who lived in Scandinavia, and the Germans who dwelt north of Italy and east of Gaul. The nature of the northern country was such that the people could not get a living by peaceful agriculture. So it was natural that in the intervals of cattle-tending they should explore the seas all about, and ravage neighboring lands. The Romans and the Gauls experienced this in the centuries just before and after Christ, and England from the eighth to the tenth centuries. Such a life made the Norsemen adventurous, hardy, warlike, independent, and quick of action, while the Celts were by nature more slothful and fond of peaceful social gatherings, though of quicker intellect and wit.

Like the Greeks and Romans, the Teutons had twelve gods and goddesses, among whom were Odin or Wotan, the king, and his wife Freya, queen of Beauty and love. Idun guarded the apples of immortality, which the gods ate to keep them eternally young. The chief difference in Teutonic mythology was the presence of an evil god, Loki. Like Vulcan, Loki was a god of fire, like him, Loki was lame because he had been cast out of heaven. Loki was always plotting against the other gods, as Lucifer, after being banished from Heaven by God, plotted against him and his people, and became Satan, "the enemy."

"Him the Almighty Power
Hurl'd headlong flaming from th' ethereal
sky

With hideous ruin and combustion down
To bottomless perdition, there to dwell
In adamantine chains and penal fire,
Who durst defy th' Omnipotent to arms."
—MILTON: *Paradise Lost.*

It was this god of evil in Teutonic myth who
was responsible for the death of the bright beautiful
sun-god, Baldur. Mistletoe was the only thing in the
world which had not sworn not to harm Baldur.
Loki knew this, and gave a twig of mistletoe to
Baldur's blind brother, Hodur, and Hodur cast it at
Baldur and "unwitting slew" him. Vali, a younger
brother of Baldur, avenged him by killing Hodur.
Hodur is darkness and Baldur light; they are
brothers; the light falls a victim to blind darkness,
who reigns until a younger brother, the sun of the
next day, rises to slay him in turn.

Below these gods, all nature was peopled
with divinities. There were elves of two kinds:
black elves, called trolls, who were frost spirits, and
guarded treasure (seeds) in the ground; and white
elves, who lived in mid-heaven, and danced on the
earth in fairy rings, where a mortal entering died.
Will-o'-the-wisps hovered over swamps to mislead
travellers, and jack-o'-lanterns, the spirits of
murderers, walked the earth near the places of their
crimes.

The Otherworlds of the Teutons were
Valhalla, the abode of the heroes whom death had
found on the battlefield, and Niflheim, "the misty

realm," secure from the cold outside, ruled over by Queen Hel. Valkyries, warlike women who rode through the air on swift horses, seized the heroes from the field of slaughter, and took them to the halls of Valhalla, where they enjoyed daily combats, long feasts, and drinking-bouts, music and story-telling.

The sacred tree of the Druids was the oak; that of the Teutonic priests the ash. The flat disk of earth was believed to be supported by a great ash-tree, Yggdrasil,

> "An ash know I standing,
> Named Yggdrasil,
> A stately tree sprinkled
> With water the purest;
> Thence come the dewdrops
> That fall in the dales;
> Ever-blooming, it stands
> O'er the Urdar-fountain."
> —*Voluspa saga.* (Blackwell trans.)

guarded by three fates, Was, Will, and Shall Be. The name of Was means the past, of Will, the power, howbeit small, which men have over present circumstances, and Shall Be, the future over which man has no control. Vurdh, the name of the latter, gives us the word "weird," which means fate or fateful. The three Weird Sister in Macbeth are seeresses.

Besides the ash, other trees and shrubs were believed to have peculiar powers, which they have kept, with some changes of meaning, to this day. The elder (elves' grave), the hawthorn, and the juniper, were sacred to supernatural powers.

The priests of the Teutons sacrificed prisoners of war in consecrated groves, to Tyr, god of the sword. The victims were not burned alive, as by the Druids, but cut and torn terribly, and their dead bodies burned. From these sacrifices auspices were taken. A man's innocence or guilt was manifested by gods to men through ordeals by fire; walking upon red-hot ploughshares, holding a heated bar of iron, or thrusting the hands into red-hot gauntlets, or into boiling water. If after a certain number of days no burns appeared the person was declared innocent. If a suspected man, thrown into the water, floated, he was guilty; if he sank, he was acquitted.

The rites of the Celts were done in secret, and it was forbidden that they be written down. Those of the Teutons were commemorated in Edda and Saga (poetry and prose).

In the far north the shortness of summer and the length of winter so impressed the people that when they made a story about it they told of a maiden, the Spring, put to sleep, and guarded, along with a hoard of treasure, by a ring of fire. One knight only could break through the flames, awaken her and seize the treasure. He is the returning sun, and the treasure he gets possession of is the wealth of summer vegetation. So there is the story of Brynhild, pricked by the "sleep-thorn" of her father, Wotan, and sleeping until Sigurd wakens her. They marry, but soon Sigurd has to give her up to Gunnar, the relentless winter, and Gunnar cannot rest until he has killed Sigurd, and reigns undisturbed. Grimm's story of Rapunzel, the princess who was shut up by a winter witch, and of Briar-Rose, pricked by a witch's spindle, and sleeping inside a hedge which blooms with spring at the knight's approach, mean likewise the struggle between summer and winter.

The chief festivals of the Teutonic year were held at Midsummer and Midwinter. May-Day, the very beginning of spring, was celebrated by May-ridings, when winter and spring, personified by two warriors, engaged in a combat in which Winter, the fur-clad king of ice and snow, was defeated. It was then that the sacred fire had been kindled, and the sacrificial feast held. Judgements were rendered then.

The summer solstice was marked by bonfires, like those of the Celts on May Eve and Midsummer. They were kindled in an open place or on a hill, and the ceremonies held about them were similar to the Celtic. As late as the eighteenth century these same customs were observed in Iceland.

A May-pole wreathed with magical herbs is erected as the center of the dance in Sweden, and in Norway a child chosen May-bride is followed by a procession as at a real wedding. This is a symbol of the wedding of sun and earth deities in the spring. The May-pole, probably imported from Celtic countries, is used at Midsummer because the spring does not begin in the north before June.

Yule-tide in December celebrated the sun's turning back, and was marked by banquets and gayety. A chief feature of all these feasts was the drinking of toasts to the gods, with vows and prayers.

By the sixth century Christianity had supplanted Druidism in the British Isles. It was the ninth before Christianity made much progress in

Scandinavia. After King Olaf had converted his nation, the toasts which had been drunk to the pagan gods were kept in honor of Christian saints; for instance, those to Freya were now drunk to the Virgin Mary or to St. Gertrude.

The "wetting of the sark-sleeve," that custom of Scotland and Ireland, was in its earliest form a rite to Freya as the northern goddess of love. To secure her aid in a love-affair, a maid would wash in a running stream a piece of fine linen—for Freya was fond of personal adornment—and would hang it before the fire to dry an hour before midnight. At half-past eleven she must turn it, and at twelve her lover's apparition would appear to her, coming in at the half-open door.

"The wind howled through the leafless boughs, and there was every appearance of an early and severe winter, as indeed befell. Long before eleven o'clock all was hushed and quiet within the house, and indeed without (nothing was heard), except the cold wind which howled mournfully in gusts. The house was an old farmhouse, and we sat in the large kitchen with its stone floor, awaiting the first stroke of the eleventh hour. It struck at last, and then all pale and trembling we hung the garment before the fire which we had piled up with wood, and set the door ajar, for that was an essential point. The door was lofty and opened upon the farm- yard, through which there was a kind of thoroughfare, very seldom used, it is true, and at each end of it there was a gate by which wayfarers occasionally passed to shorten the way. There we sat without speaking a word, shivering with cold and fear, listening to the clock which went slowly, tick, tick, and occasionally starting as the door creaked on its hinges, or a half-burnt billet fell upon the hearth. My sister was ghastly white, as white as the garment which was drying before the fire. And how half an hour had elapsed and it was time to turn. . . . This we did, I and my sister, without saying a word, and then we again sank on our chairs on either side of the fire. I was tired, and as the clock went tick-a-tock, I began to feel myself dozing. I did doze, I believe. All of a sudden I sprang up. The clock was striking one, two, but ere it could give the third chime, mercy upon us! we heard the gate slam with a tremendous noise. . . ."

"Well, and what happened then?"

"Happened! before I could recover myself, my sister had sprung to the door, and both locked and bolted it. The next moment she was in convulsions. I scarcely knew what happened; and yet it appeared to me for a moment that something pressed against the door with a low moaning sound. Whether it was the wind or not, I can't say. I shall never forget that night. About two hours later, my father came home. He had been set upon by a highwayman whom he beat off."

—BORROW: *Lavengro.*

Freya and Odin especially had had power over the souls of the dead. When Christianity turned all the old gods into spirits of evil, these two were accused especially of possessing unlawful learning, as having knowledge of the hidden matters of death. This unlawful wisdom is the first accusation that has always been brought against witches. A mirror is often used to contain it. Such are the crystals of the astrologers, and the looking-glasses which on

Hallowe'en materialize wishes.

From that time in the Middle Ages when witches were first heard of, it has nearly always been women who were accused. Women for the most part were the priests in the old days: it was a woman to whom Apollo at Delphi breathed his oracles. In all times it has been women who plucked herbs and concocted drinks of healing and refreshment. So it was very easy to imagine that they experimented with poisons and herbs of magic power under the guidance of the now evil gods. If they were so directed, they must go on occasions to consult with their masters. The idea arose of a witches' Sabbath, when women were enabled by evil means to fly away, and adore in secret the gods from whom the rest of the world had turned. There were such meeting-places all over Europe. They had been places of sacrifice, of judgement, or of wells and springs considered holy under the old religion, and whither the gods had now been banished. The most famous was the Blocksberg in the Hartz mountains in Germany.

"Dame Baubo first, to lead the cerw!
A tough old sow and the mother thereon,
Then follow the witches, every one."
—GOETHE: *Faust.* (Taylor trans.)

In Norway the mountains above Bergen were a resort, and the Dovrefeld, once the home of the trolls.

"It's easy to slip in here,
But outward the Dovre-King's gate opens not."
—IBSEN: *Peer Gynt.* (Archer trans.)

In Italy the witches met under a walnut tree near Benevento; in France, in Puy de Dome; in

Spain, near Seville.

In these night-ridings Odin was the leader of a wild hunt. In stormy, blustering autumn weather.

"The wonted roar was up among the woods."

—MILTON: *Comus.*

Odin rode in pursuit of shadowy deer with the Furious Host behind him. A ghostly huntsman of a later age was Dietrich von Bern, doomed to hunt till the Judgement Day.

Frau Venus in Wagner's Tannhauser held her revels in an underground palace in the Horselberg in Thuringia, Germany. This was one of the seats of Holda, the goddess of spring. Venus herself is like the Christian conception of Freya and Hel. She gathers about her a throng of nymphs, sylphs, and those she has lured into the mountain by intoxicating music and promises. "The enchanting sounds enticed only those in whose hearts wild sensuous longings had already taken root." Of these Tannhauser is one. He has stayed a year, but it seems to him only one day. Already he is tired of the rosy light and eternal music and languor, and longs for the fresh green world of action he once knew. He fears that he has forfeited his soul's salvation by being there at all, but cries,

"Salvation rests for me in Mary!"

—WAGNER: *Tannhauser.*

At the holy name Venus and her revellers vanish, and Tannhauser finds himself in a meadow, hears the tinkling herd-bells, and a shepherd's voice singing,

"Frau Holda, goddess of the spring,
Steps forth from the mountains old;

She comes, and all the brooklets sing,
And fled is winter's cold.
* * * * *

Play, play, my pipe, your lightest lay,
For spring has come, and merry May!"
—*Tannhauser.* (Huckel trans.)
praising the goddess in her blameless state.

By the fifteenth century Satan, taking the
place of the gods, assumed control of the evil
creatures. Now that witches were the followers of
the Devil, they wrote their names in his book, and
were carried away by him for the revels by night. A
new witch was pricked with a needle to initiate her
into his company. At the party the Devil was adored
with worship due to God alone. Dancing, a device
of the pagans, and hence considered wholly wicked,
was indulged in to unseemly lengths. In 1883 in
Sweden it was believed that dances were held about
the sanctuaries of the ancient gods, and that
whoever stopped to watch were caught by the
dancers and whirled away. If they profaned holy
days by this dancing, they were doomed to keep it
up for a year.

At the witches' Sabbath the Devil himself
sometimes appeared as a goat, and the witches were
attended b cats, owls, bats, and cuckoos, because
these creatures had once been sacred to Freya. At
the fest horse-flesh, once the food of the gods at
banquets, was eaten. The broth for the feast was
brewed in a kettle held over the fire by a tripod, like
that which supported the seat of Apollo's priestess
at Delphi. The kettle may be a reminder of the one
Thor got, which gave to each guest whatever food
he asked of it, or it may be merely that used in
brewing the herb-remedies which women made

before they were thought to practise witchcraft. In the kettle were cooked mixtures which caused storms and shipwrecks, plagues, and blights. No salt was eaten, for that was a wholesome substance.

The witches of Germany did not have prophetic power; those of Scandinavia, like the Norse Fates, did have it. The troll-wives of Scandinavia were like the witches of Germany— they were cannibals, especially relishing children, like the witch in Hansel and Grethel.

For the fourteenth to the eighteenth century all through Europe and the new world people though to be witches, and hence in the devil's service, were persecuted. It was believed that they were able to take the form of beasts. A wolf or other animal is caught in a trap or shot, and disappears. Later an old woman who lives alone in the woods is found suffering from a similar wound. She is then declared to be a witch.

> "There was once an old castle in the middle
> of a vast thick wood; in it lived an old
woman
> quite alone, and she was a witch. By day she
> made herself into a cat or a screech-owl, but
> regularly at night she became a human being
> again."
> —GRIMM: *Jorinda and Joringel.*

"Hares found on May morning are witches and should be stoned," reads an old superstition. "If you tease a cat on May Eve, it will turn into a witch and hurt you."

Chapter XIII. Walpurgis Night

WALPURGA was a British nun who went to Germany in the eighth century to found holy houses. After a pious life she was buried at Eichstatt, where it is said a healing oil trickled from her rock-tomb. This miracle reminded men of the fruitful dew which fell from the manes of the Valkyries' horses, and when one of the days sacred to her came on May first, the wedding-day of Frau Holda and the sun-god, the people thought of her as a Valkyrie, and identified her with Holda. As, like a Valkyrie, she rode armed on her steed, she scattered, like Holda, spring flowers and fruitful dew upon the fields and vales. When these deities fell into disrepute, Walpurga too joined the pagan train that swept the sky on the eve of May first, and met afterwards on mountain-tops to sacrifice and adore Holda, as the priests had sacrificed for a prosperous season and a bountiful harvest.   So this night was called Walpurgis Night, when evil beings were abroad, and with them human worshippers who still guarded the old faith in secret.

This is very like the occasion of November Eve, which shared with May first Celtic manifestations of evil. Witches complete the list of supernatural beings which are out on Hallowe'en. All are to be met at crossroads, with harm to the beholders. A superstition goes, that if one wishes to see witches, he must put on his clothes wrong side out, and creep backward to a crossroads, or wear wild radish, on May Eve.

On Walpurgis Night precaution must be

taken against witches who may harm cattle. The stable doors are locked and sealed with three crosses. Sprigs of ash, hawthorn, juniper, and elder, once sacred to the pagan gods, are now used as a protection against them.

Horseshoes are nailed prongs up on the threshold or over the door. Holy bells are hung on the cows to scare away the witches, and they are guided to pasture by a goad which has been blessed. Shots are fired over the cornfield. If one wishes, he may hide in the corn and hear what will happen for a year.

Signs and omens on Walpurgis Night have more weight that at other times except on St. John's Day.

"On Walpurgis Night rain
Makes good crops of autumn grain,"
but rain on May Day is harmful to them.

Lovers try omens on this eve, as they do in Scotland on Hallowe'en. If you sleep with one stocking on, you will find on May morning in the toe a hair the color of your sweetheart's. Girls try to find out the temperament of their husbands-to-be by keeping a linen thread for three days near an image of the Madonna, and at midnight on May Eve pulling it apart, saying:

"Thread, I pull thee;
Walpurga, I pray thee,
That thou show to me
What my husband's like to be."

They judge of his disposition by the thread's being strong or easily broken, soft or tightly woven.

Dew on the morning of May first makes girls who wash in it beautiful.

"The fair maid who on the first of May
Goes to the fields at break of day
And washes in dew from the hawthorn tree
Will ever after handsome be."
—*Encyclopedia of Superstitions.*

A heavy dew on this morning presages a good "butter-year." You will find fateful initials printed in dew on a handkerchief that has been left out all the night of April thirtieth.

On May Day girls invoke the cuckoo:
"Cuckoo! cuckoo! on the bough,
Tell me truly, tell me how
Many years there will be
Till a husband comes to me."

Then they count the calls of the cuckoo until he pauses again.

If a man wears clothes made of yarn spun on Walpurgis Night to the May-shooting, he will always hit the bull's-eye, for the Devil gives away to those he favors, "freikugeln," bullets which always hit the mark.

On Walpurgis Night as on Hallowe'en strange things may happen to one. Zschokke tells a story of a Walpurgis Night dream that is more a vision than a dream. Led to be unfaithful to his wife, a man murders the husband of a former sweetheart; to escape capture he fires a haystack, from which a whole village is kindled. In his flight he enters an empty carriage, and drives away madly, crushing the owner under the wheels. He finds that the dead man is his own brother. Faced by the person whom he believes to be the Devil, responsible for his misfortunes, the wretched man is ready to worship him if he will protect him. He finds that the seeming Devil is in reality his guardian-angel who sent him this dream that he might learn the depths of wickedness lying unfathomed in his heart, waiting an opportunity to burst out.

Both May Eve and St. John's Eve are times of freedom and unrestraint. People are filled with a sort of madness which makes them unaccountable for their deeds.

"For you see, pastor, within every one of us a spark of paganism is glowing. It has out-lasted the thousand years since the old Teutonic times. Once a year is flames up high, and we call it St. John's Fire. Once a year comes Free-night. Yes, truly, Free-night. Then the witches, laughing scornfully, ride to Blocksberg, upon the mountain-top, on their broomsticks, the same broomsticks with which at other times their witchcraft is whipped out of them,—then the whole wild company skims along the forest way,—and then the wild desires awaken in our hearts which life has not fulfilled."

—SUDERMANN: *St. John's Fire.* (Porter trans.)

Chapter XIV. More Hallowtide Beliefs and Customs

ONLY the Celts and the Teutonics celebrate an occasion actually like our Hallowe'en. The countries of southern Europe make of it a religious vigil, like that already described in France. In Italy on the night of All Souls', the spirits of the dead are thought to be abroad, as in Brittany. They may mingle with living people, and not be remarked. The Miserere is heard in all the cities. As the people pass dressed in black, bells are rung on street corners to remind them to pray for the souls of the dead. In Naples the skeletons in the funeral vaults are dressed up, and the place visited on All Souls' Day. In Salerno before the people go to the all-night services at church they set out a banquet for the dead. If any food is left in the morning, evil is in store for the house.

"Hark! Hark to the wind! 'T is the night, they say,
When all souls come back from the far away—
The dead, forgotten this many a day!
"And the dead remembered—ay! long and well—
And the little children whose spirits dwell
In God's green garden of asphodel.
"Have you reached the country of all content,
O souls we know, since the day you went

From this time-worn world, where your
years were spent?
　　"Would you come back to the sun and the
rain,
　　The sweetness, the strife, the thing we call
pain,
　　And then unravel life's tangle again?
　　"I lean to the dark—Hush!—was it a sigh?
　　Or the painted vine-leaves that rustled by?
　　Or only a night-bird's echoing cry?"
　　—SHEARD: *Hallowe'en.*

In Malta bells are rung, prayers said, and
mourning worn on All Souls' Day. Graves are
decorated, and the inscriptions on tombs read and
reread. For the poor is prepared an All Souls'
dinner, as cakes are given to the poor in England
and Wales. The custom of decorating graves with
flowers and offering flowers to the dead comes
from the crowning of the dead by the ancients with
short-lived blooms, to signify the brevity of life.

In Spain at dark on Hallowe'en cakes and
nuts are laid on graves to bribe the spirits not to
disturb the vigils of the saints.

In Germany the graves of the dead are
decorated with flowers and lights, on the first and
second of November. To drive away ghosts from a
church a key or a wand must be struck three times
against a bier. An All Souls' divination in Germany
is a girl's going out and asking the first young man
she meets his name. Her husband's will be like it. If
she walks thrice about a church and makes a wish,
she will see it fulfilled.

Belgian children build shrines in front of
their homes with figures of the Madonna and

candles, and beg for money to buy cakes. As many cakes as one eats, so many souls he frees from Purgatory.

The races of northern Europe believed that the dead returned, and were grieved at the lamentations of their living relatives. The same belief was found in Brittany, and among the American Indians.

> "Think of this, O Hiawatha!
> Speak of it to all the people,
> That henceforward and forever
> They no more with lamentations
> Sadden souls of the departed
> In the Islands of the Blessed!"
> —LONGFELLOW: *Hiawatha.*

The Chinese fear the dead and the dragons of the air. They devote the first three weeks in April to visiting the graves of their ancestors, and laying baskets of offerings on them. The great dragon, Feng-Shin, flies scattering blessings upon the houses. His path is straight, unless he meets with some building. Then he turns aside, and the owner of the too lofty edifice misses the blessing.

At Nikko, Japan, where there are many shrines to the spirits of the dead, masques are held to entertain the ghosts who return on Midsummer Day. Every street is lined with lighted lanterns, and the spirits are sent back to the otherworld in straw boats lit with lanterns, and floated down the river. To see ghosts in Japan one must put one hundred rush-lights into a large lantern, and repeat one hundred lines of poetry, taking one light out at the end of each line; or go out into the dark with one light and blow it out. Ghosts are identified with witches. They come back especially on moonlit nights.

> "On moonlight nights, when the coast-wind
> whispers in the branches of the tree, O-
Matsue
> and Teoyo may sometimes be seen, with
bamboo
> racks in their hands, gathering together the
> needles of the fir."
> —RINDER: *Great Fir-Tree of Takasago.*

There is a Chinese saying that a mirror is the soul of a woman. A pretty story is told of a girl whose mother before she died gave her a mirror, saying:

"Now after I am dead, if you think longingly of me, take out the thing that you will find inside this box, and look at it. When you do so my spirit will meet yours, and you will be comforted." When she was lonely or her stepmother was harsh with her, the girl went to her room and looked earnestly into the mirror. She saw there only her own face, but it was so much like her mother's that she believed it was hers indeed, and was consoled. When the stepmother learned what it was her daughter cherished so closely, her heart softened toward the lonely girl, and her life was made easier.

By the Arabs spirits were called Djinns (or genii). They came from fire, and looked like men or beasts. They might be good or evil, beautiful or horrible, and could disappear from mortal sight at will. Nights when they were abroad, it behooved men to stay under cover.

"Ha! They are on us, close without!
Shut tight the shelter where we lie;
With hideous din the monster rout,
Dragon and vampire, fill the sky."
—HUGO: *The Djinns*.

Chapter XV. Hallowe'en in America

IN Colonial days Hallowe'en was not celebrated
much in America. Some English still kept the
customs of the old world, such as apple-ducking
and snapping, and girls tried the apple-paring charm
to reveal their lovers' initials, and the comb-and-
mirror test to see their faces. Ballads were sung and
ghost-stories told, for the dead were thought to
return on Hallowe'en.

"There was a young officer in Phip's
company at the time of the finding of the Spanish
treasure-ship, who had gone mad at the sight of the
bursting sacks that the divers had brought up from
the sea, as the gold coins covered the deck. This
man had once lived in the old stone house on the
'faire greene lane,' and a report had gone out that his
spirit still visited it, and caused discordant noises.
Once . . . on a gusty November evening, when the
clouds were scudding over the moon, a hall-door
had blown open with a shrieking draft and a force
that caused the floor to tremble."

—BUTTERWORTH: *Hallowe'en
Reformation.*

Elves, goblins, and fairies are native on
American soil. The Indians believed in evil
manitous, some of whom were water-gods who
exacted tribute from all who passed over their lakes.
Henry Hudson and his fellow-explorers haunted as
mountain-trolls the Catskill range. Like Ossian and
so many other visitors to the Otherworld, Rip Van
Winkle is lured into the strange gathering, thinks

that he passes the night there, wakes, and goes home to find that twenty years have whitened his hair, rusted his gun, and snatched from life many of his boon-companions.

"My gun must have cotched the rheumatix too. Now that's too bad. Them fellows have gone and stolen my good gun, and leave me this rusty old barrel.

"Why, is that the village of Falling Waters that I see? Why, the place is more than twice the size it was last night—I—

"I don't know whether I am dreaming, or sleeping, or waking."
—JEFFERSON: *Rip Van Winkle.*

The persecution of witches, prevalent in Europe, reached this side of the Atlantic in the seventeenth century.

"This sudden burst of wickedness and crime
Was but the common madness of the time,
When in all lands, that lie within the sound
Of Sabbath bells, a witch was burned or drowned."
—LONGFELLOW: *Giles Corey of the Salem Farms.*

Men and women who had enemies to accuse them of evil knowledge and the power to cause illness in others, were hanged or pressed to death by heavy weights. Such sicknesses they could cause by keeping a waxen image, and sticking pins or nails into it, or melting it before the fire. The person whom they hated would be in torture, or would waste away like the waxen doll. Witches' power to injure and to prophesy came from the Devil, who marked them with a needle-prick. Such marks were sought as evidence at trials.

"Witches' eyes are coals of fire from the pit." They were attended by black cats, owls, bats, and toads.

Iron, as being a product of fire, was a protection against them , as against evil spirits everywhere. It had especial power when in the shape of a horseshoe.

"This horseshoe will I nail upon the threshold.
There, ye night-hags and witches that torment
The neighborhood, ye shall not enter here."
—LONGFELLOW: *Giles Corey of the Salem Farms.*

The holiday-time of elves, witches, and ghosts is Hallowe'en. It is not believed in here except by some children, who people the dark with bogies who will carry them away if they are naughty.

"Onc't they was a little boy wouldn't say his prayers—
An' when he went to bed at night, away upstairs,
His mammy heerd him holler, an' his daddy heerd him bawl,
An' when they turn't the kivvers down, he wasn't there at all!
An' they seeked him in the rafter-room, an'

cubby-hole, an' press,

An' seeked him up the chimbley-flue, an'
ever'wheres, I guess;

But all they ever found was thist his pants
an' roundabout!

An' the Gobble-uns 'll git you, ef you don't
watch out!"

—RILEY: *Little Orphant Annie.*

Negroes are very superstitious, putting faith
in all sorts of supernatural beings.

"Blame my trap! how de wind do blow;

And dis is das de night for de witches, sho!

Dey's trouble going to waste when de ole
slut whine,

An' you hear de cat a-spittin' when de moon
don't shine."

—RILEY: *When de Folks is Gone.*

While the original customs of Hallowe'en
are being forgotten more and more across the ocean,
Americans have fostered them, and are making this
an occasion something like what it must have been
in its best days overseas. All Hallowe'en customs in
the United States are borrowed directly or adapted
from those of other countries. All superstitions,
everyday ones, and those pertaining to Christmas
and New Year's, have special value on Hallowe'en.

It is a night of ghostly and merry revelry.
Mischievous spirits choose it for carrying off gates
and other objects, and hiding them or putting them
out of reach.

"Dear me, Polly, I wonder what them boys

will be up to-night. I do hope they'll not put

the gate up on the shed as they did last year."

—WRIGHT: *Tom's Hallowe'en Joke.*

Bags filled with flour sprinkle the passers-by. Door-bells are rung and mysterious raps sounded on doors, things thrown into halls, and knobs stolen. Such sports mean no more at Hallowe'en than the tricks played the night before the Fourth of July have to do with the Declaration of Independence. We see manifested on all such occasions the spirit of "Free-night" of which George von Hartwig speaks so enthusiastically in St. John's Fire (page 141).

Hallowe'en parties are the real survival of the ancient merrymakings. They are prepared for in secret. Guests are not to divulge the fact that they are invited. Often they come masked, as ghosts or witches.

The decorations make plain the two elements of the festival. For the centerpiece of the table there may be a hollowed pumpkin, filled with apples and nuts and other fruits of harvest, or a pumpkin-chariot drawn by field-mice. So it is clear that this is a harvest-party, like Pomona's feast. In the coach rides a witch, representing the other element, of magic and prophesy. Jack-o'-lanterns, with which the room is lighted, are hollowed pumpkins with candles inside. The candlelight shines through holes cut like features. So the lantern becomes a bogy, and is held up at a window to frighten those inside. Cornstalks from the garden stand in clomps about the room. A frieze of witches on broomsticks, with cats, bats, and owls surmounts the fireplace, perhaps. A full moon shines over all, and a caldron on a tripod holds fortunes tied in nutshells. The prevailing colors are yellow and black; a deep yellow is the color of most ripe grain and fruit; black stands for black magic and demoniac influence. Ghosts and skulls and cross-bones, symbols of death, startle the beholder. Since Hallowe'en is a time for lovers to learn their fate, hearts and other sentimental tokens are used to good effect, as the Scotch lads of Burns's time wore love-knots.

Having marched to the dining-room to the time of a dirge, the guests find before them plain, hearty fare; doughnuts, gingerbread, cider, popcorn, apples, and nuts honored by time. The Hallowe'en cake had held the place of honor since the beginning here in America. A ring, key, thimble, penny, and button baked in it foretell respectively speedy marriage, a jouney, spinsterhood, wealth, and bachelorhood.

"Polly was going to be married, Jennie was going on a long journey, and you—down went the knife against something hard. The girls crowded round. You had a hurt in your throat, and there, there, in your slice, was the horrid, hateful, big brass thimble. It was more than you could bear—soaking, dripping wet, and an old maid!"
—BRADLEY: *Different Party.*

The kitchen is the best place for the rough games and after-supper charms.

On the stems of the apples which are to be dipped for may be tied names; for the boys in one tub, for the girls in another. Each searcher of the future must draw out with his teeth an apple with a name which will be like that of his future mate.

A variation of the Irish snap-apple is a hoop hung by strings from the ceiling, round which at intervals are placed bread, apples, cakes, peppers, candies, and candles. The strings are twisted, then let go, and as the hoop revolves, each may step up and get a bite from whatever comes to him. By the taste he determines what the character of his married life will be,—whether wholesome, acid, soft, fiery, or sweet. Whoever bites the candle is twice unfortunate, for he must pay a forfeit too. An apple and a bag of flour are placed on the ends of a stick, and whoever dares to seize a mouthful of apple must risk being blinded by flour. Apples are suspended one to a string in a doorway. As they swing, each guest tries to secure his apple. To blow out a candle as it revolves on a stick requires attention and accuracy of aim.

The one who first succeeds in threading a needle as he sits on a round bottle on the floor will be first married. Twelve candles are lighted, and placed at convenient distances on the floor in a row. As the guest leaps over them, the first he blows out will indicate his wedding-month. One candle only placed on the floor and blown out in the same way means a year of wretchedness ahead. If it still burns, it presages a year of joy.

Among the quieter tests some of the most common are tried with apple-seeds. As in England a pair of seeds named for two lovers are stuck on brow or eyelids. The one who sticks longer is the true, the one who soon falls, the disloyal sweetheart. Seeds are used in this way to tell also whether one is to be a traveler or a stay-at-home. Apple-seeds are twice ominous, partaking of both apple and nut nature. Even the number of seeds found in a core has meaning. If you put them upon the palm of your hand, and strike it with the other, the number remaining will tell you how many letters you will receive in a fortnight. With twelve seeds and the names of twelve friends, the old rhyme may be repeated:

> "One I love,
> Two I love,
> Three I love, I say;
> Four I love with all my heart:
> Five I cast away.
> Six he loves,
> Seven she loves,
> Eight they both love;
> Nine he comes,
> Ten he tarries,
> Eleven he courts, and
> Twelve he marries."

Nuts are burned in the open fire. It is generally agreed that the one for whom the first that pops is named, loves.

> "If he loves me, pop and fly;
> If he hates me, live and die."

Often the superstition connected therewith is forgotten in the excitement of the moment.

> "When ebery one among us toe de smallest pickaninny
> Would huddle in de chimbley cohnah's glow,
> Toe listen toe dem chilly win's ob ole Novembah's
> Go a-screechin' lack a spook around de huts,

'Twell de pickaninnies' fingahs gits to
shakin' o'er de embahs,
An' dey laik ter roas' dey knuckles 'stead o'
nuts."
—IN WERNER'S *Readings,* Number 31.

Letters of the alphabet are carved on a
pumpkin. Fate guides the hand of the blindfolded
seeker to the fateful initial which he stabs with a
pin. Letters cut out of paper are sprinkled on water
in a tub. They form groups from which any one with
imagination may spell out names.
Girls walk down cellar backward with a
candle in one hand and a looking-glass in the other,
expecting to see a face in the glass.

"Last night 't was witching Hallowe'en,
Dearest; an apple russet-brown
I pared, and thrice above my crown
Whirled the long skin; they watched it keen;
I flung it far; they laughed and cried me
shame—
Dearest, there lay the letter of your name.
"Took I the mirror then, and crept
Down, down the creaking narrow stair;
The milk-pans caught my candle's flare
And mice walked soft and spiders slept.
I spoke the spell, and stood the magic space,
Dearest—and in the glass I saw your face!
"And then I stole out in the night
Alone; the frogs piped sweet and loud,
The moon looked through a ragged cloud.
Thrice round the house I sped me light,
Dearest; and there, methought—charm of
my charms!

You met me, kissed me, took me to your arms!"
—OPPER: *The Charms.*

There are many mirror tests. A girl who sits before a mirror at midnight on Hallowe'en combing her hair and eating an apple will see the face of her true love reflected in the glass. Standing so that through a window she may see the moon in a glass she holds, she counts the number of reflections to find out how many pleasant things will happen to her in the next twelve months. Alabama has taken over the Scotch mirror test in its entirety.

A girl with a looking-glass in her hand steps backward from the door out into the yard. Saying:
"Round and round, O stars so fair!
Ye travel, and search out everywhere.
I pray you, sweet stars, now show to me,
This night, who my future husband shall be!"
she goes to meet her fate.

"So Leslie backed out at the door, and we shut it upon her. The instant after, we heard a great laugh. Off the piazza she had stepped backward directly against two gentlemen coming in.

"Doctor Ingleside was one, coming to get his supper; the other was a friend of his. . . .

'Doctor John Hautayne,' he said, introducing him by his full name."
—WHITNEY: *We Girls.*

A custom that is a reminder of the lighted boats sent down-stream in Japan to bear away the souls of the dead, is that which makes use of nutshell boats. These have tiny candles fastened in them, are lighted, and named, and set adrift on a tub of water. If they cling to the side, their namesakes will lead a quiet life. Some will float together. Some will bear steadily toward a goal thou the waves are rocked in a tempest. Their behavior is significant. The candle which burns longest belongs to the one who will marry first.

The Midsummer wheel which was rolled down into the Moselle River in France, and meant, if the flames that wreathed it were not extinguished, that the grape-harvest would be abundant, has survived in the fortune wheel which is rolled about from one guest to another, and brings a gift to each.

The actions of cats on Hallowe'en betoken good or bad luck. If a cat sits quietly beside any one, he will enjoy a peaceful, prosperous life; if one rubs against him, it brings good luck, doubly good if one jumps into his lap. If a cat yawns near you on Hallowe'en, be alert and do not let opportunity slip by you. If a cat runs from you, you have a secret which will be revealed in seven days.

Different states have put interpretations of their own on the commonest charms. In Massachusetts the one who first draws an apple from the tub with his teeth will be first married. If a girl steals a cabbage, she will see her future husband as she pulls it up, or meet him as she goes home. If these fail, she must put the cabbage over the door and watch to see whom it falls on, for him she is to marry. A button concealed in mashed potato brings misfortune to the finder. The names of three men are written on slips of paper, and enclosed in three balls of meal. The one that rises first when they are thrown into water will disclose the sought-for name.

Maine has borrowed the yarn-test from Scotland. A ball is thrown into a barn or cellar, and wound off on the hand. The lover will come and help to wind. Girls in New Hampshire place in a row three dishes with earth, water, and a ring in them, respectively. The one who blindfolded touches earth will soon die; water, will never marry; the ring, will soon be wedded.

To dream of the future on Hallowe'en in Pennsylvania, one must go out of the front door backward, pick up dust or grass, wrap it in paper, and put it under his pillow.

In Maryland girls see their future husbands by a rite similar to the Scotch "wetting of the sark-sleeve." They put an egg to a roast, and open wide all the doors and windows. The man they seek will come in and turn the egg. At supper girls stand behind the chairs, knowing that the ones they are to marry will come to sit in front of them.

The South has always been famous for its hospitality and good times. On Hallowe'en a miniature Druid-fire burns in a bowl on the table. In the blazing alcohol are put furtunes wrapped in tin-foil, figs, orange-peel, raisins, almonds, and dates. The one who snatches the best will meet his sweetheart inside of a year, and all may try for a fortune from the flames. The origin of this custom was the taking of omens from the death-struggles of creatures burning in the fire of sacrifice.

Another Southern custom is adapted from one of Brittany. Needles are named and floated in a dish of water. Those which cling side by side are lovers.

Good fortune is in store for the one who

wins an apple from the tub, or against whose glass a
ring suspended by a hair strikes with a sharp chime.

A very elaborate charm is tried in
Newfoundland. As the clock strikes midnight a girl
puts the twenty-six letters of the alphabet, cut from
paper, into a pure-white bowl which has been
touched by the lips of a new-born babe only. After
saying:

> "Kind fortune, tell me where is he
> Who my future lore shall be;
> From this bowl all that I claim
> Is to know my sweetheart's name."

she puts the bowl into a safe place until
morning. Then she is blindfolded and picks out the
same number of letters as there are in her own
name, and spells another from them.

In New Brunswick, instead of an apple, a
hard-boiled egg without salt is eaten before a
mirror, with the same result. In Canada a thread is
held over a lamp. The number that can be counted
slowly before the thread parts, is the number of
years before the one who counts will marry.

In the United States a hair is thrown to the
winds with the stanza chanted:

> "I pluck this lock of hair off my head
> To tell whence comes the one I shall wed.
> Fly, silken hair, fly all the world around,
> Until you reach the spot where my true love
is found."

The direction in which the hair floats is
prophetic.

The taste in Hallowe'en festivities now is to
study old traditions, and hold a Scotch party, using
Burn's poem Hallowe'en as a guide; or to go a-
souling as the English used. In short, no custom that

was once honored at Hallowe'en is out of fashion now. "Cyniver" has been borrowed from Wales, and the "dumb-cake" from the Hebrides. In the Scotch custom of cabbage-stalk, if the stalk comes up easily, the husband or wife will be easy to win. The melted-lead test to show the occupation of the husband-to-be has been adopted in the United States. If the metal cools in round drops, the tester will never marry, or her husband will have no profession. White of egg is used in the same way. Like the Welsh test is that of filling the mouth with water, and walking round the house until one meets one's fate. An adaptation of the Scottish "three luggies" is the row of four dishes holding dirt, water, a ring, and a rag. The dirt means divorce, the water, a trip across the ocean, the ring, marriage, the rag, no marriage at all.

After the charms have been tried, fagots are passed about, and by the eerie light of burning salt and alcohol, ghost stories are told, each concluding his installment as his fagot withers into ashes. Sometimes the cabbage stalks used in the omens take the place of fagots.

To induce prophetic dreams salt, in quantities from a pinch to an egg full, is eaten before one goes to bed.

"'Miss Jeanette, that's such a fine trick! You must swallow a salt herring in three bites, bones and all, and not drink a drop till the apparition of your future spouse comes in the night to offer you a drink of water.'"

—ADAMS: *Chrissie's Fate.*

If, after taking three doses of salt two

minutes apart, a girl goes to bed backward, lies on
her right side, and does not move till morning, she
is sure to have eventful dreams. Pills made of a
hazelnut, a walnut, and nutmeg grated together and
mixed with butter and sugar cause dreams: if of
gold, the husband will be rich; if of noise, a
tradesman; if of thunder and lightning, a traveler.
As in Ireland bay-leaves on or under a man's pillow
cause him to dream of his sweetheart. Also

    "Turn your boots toward the street,

    Leave your garters on your feet,

    Put your stockings on your head,

    You'll dream of the one you're going to
wed."

    Lemon-peel carried all day and rubbed on
the bed-posts at night will cause an apparition to
bring the dreaming girl two lemons. For quiet sleep
and the fulfilment of any wish eat before going to
bed on Hallowe'en a piece of dry bread.

    A far more interesting development of the
Hallowe'en idea than these innocent but colorless
superstitions, is promised by the pageant at Fort
Worth, Texas, on October thirty-first, 1916. In the
masque and pageant of the afternoon four thousand
school children took part. At night scenes from the
pageant were staged on floats which passed along
the streets. The subject was Preparedness for Peace,
and comprised scenes from American history in
which peace played an honorable part. Such were:
the conference of William Penn and the Quakers
with the Indians, and the opening of the East to
American trade. This is not a subject limited to
performances at Hallowtide. May there not be
written and presented in America a truly Hallowe'en
pageant, illustrating and befitting its noble origin,

and making its place secure among the holidays of
the year?

Four Poems

Hallowe'en

Bring forth the raisins and the nuts—   To-
night All Hallows' Spectre struts
      Along the moonlit way.
      No time is this for tear or sob,
      Or other woes our joys to rob,
      But time for Pippin and for Bob,
      And Jack-o'-lantern gay.
      Come forth, ye lass and trousered kid,
      From prisoned mischief raise the lid,
      And lift it good and high.
      Leave grave old Wisdom in the lurch,
      Set Folly on a lofty perch,
      Nor fear the awesome rod of birch
      When dawn illumes the sky.
      'Tis night for revel, set apart
      To reillume the darkened heart,
      And rout the hosts of Dole.
      'Tis night when Goblin, Elf, and Fay,
      Come dancing in their best array
      To prank and royster on the way,

And ease the troubled soul.
The ghosts of all things, past parade,
Emerging from the mist and shade
That hid them from our gaze,
And full of song and ringing mirth,
In one glad moment of rebirth,
Again they walk the ways of earth,
As in the ancient days.
The beason light shines on the hill,
The will-o'-wisps the forests fill
With flashes filched from noon;
And witches on thier broomsticks spry
Speed here and yonder in the sky,
And lift their strident voices high
Unto the Hunter's moon.
The air resounds with tuneful notes
From myriads of straining throats,
All hailing Folly Queen;
So join the swelling choral throng,
Forget your sorrow and your wrong,
In one glad hour of joyous song
To honor Hallowe'en.
—J.K. BANGS in *Harper's Weekly,* Nov. 5,
1910.

Hallowe'en Failure

Who's dat peekin' in de do'?
Set mah heart a-beatin'!
Thought I see' a spook for sho
On mah way to meetin'.
Heerd a rustlin' all aroun',
Trees all sort o' jiggled;
An' along de frosty groun'
Funny shadders wriggled.
Who's dat by de winder-sill?
Gittin' sort o' skeery;
Feets is feelin' kind o' chill,
Eyes is sort o' teary.
'Most as nervous as a coon
When de dawgs is barkin',
Er a widder when some spoon
Comes along a-sparkin'.
Whass dat creepin' up de road,
Quiet like a ferret,
Hoppin' sof'ly as a toad?
Maybe hit's a sperrit!
Lordy! hope dey ain't no ghos'
Come to tell me howdy.
I ain't got no use for those
Fantoms damp an' cloudy.
Whass dat standin' by de fence
Wid its eyes a-yearnin',
Drivin' out mah common-sense
Wid its glances burnin'?
Don't dass skeercely go to bed
Wid dem spookses roun' me.
Ain't no res' fo' dis yere head

When dem folks surroun' me.
Whass dat groanin' soun' I hear
Off dar by de gyardin?
Lordy! Lordy! Lordy dear,
Grant dis sinner pardon!
I won't nebber—I declar'
Ef it ain't my Sammy!
Sambo, what yo' doin' dar?
Yo' can't skeer yo' mammy!
—CARLYLE SMITH in *Harper's Weekly,*
Oct. 29, 1910.

Hallowe'en

Pixie, kobold, elf, and sprite
All are on their rounds to-night,—
In the wan moon's silver ray
Thrives their helter-skelter play.
Fond of cellar, barn, or stack
True unto the almanac,
They present to credulous eyes
Strange hobgoblin mysteries.
Cabbage-stumps—straws wet with dew—
Apple-skins, and chestnuts too,
And a mirror for some lass
Show what wonders come to pass.
Doors they move, and gates they hide
Mischiefs that on moonbeams ride
Are their deeds,—and, by their spells,

Love records its oracles.
Don't we all, of long ago
By the ruddy fireplace glow,
In the kitchen and the hall,
Those queer, coof-like pranks recall?
Eery shadows were they then—
But to-night they come again;
Were we once more but sixteen
Precious would be Hallowe'en.
       —JOEL BENTON in *Harper's Weekly,* Oct.
31, 1896.

Hallowe'en

A gypsy flame in on the hearth,
Sign of this carnival of mirth.
Through the dun fields and from the glade
Flash merry folk in masquerade—
It is the witching Hallowe'en.
Pale tapers glimmer in the sky,
The dead and dying leaves go by;
Dimly across the faded green
Strange shadows, stranger shades, are
seen,—
It is the mystic Hallowe'en.
Soft gusts of love and memory
Beat at the heart reproachfully;
The lights that burn for those who die
Were flickering low, let them flare high—

It is the haunting Hallowe'en.
—A.F. MURRAY in *Harper's Weekly,* Oct. 30, 1909.

25473900R00072

Made in the USA
Middletown, DE
31 October 2015